VEDIC CONCEPT OF DHARMA
A Philosophical Analysis

VEDIC CONCEPT OF DHARMA
A Philosophical Analysis

Original Oḍiā by
DR. GANESWAR MISRA

English Rendering by
JAGANNATH DASH

MOTILAL BANARSIDASS PUBLISHERS
PRIVATE LIMITED • DELHI

First Edition : **Delhi, 2018**

ISBN: 978-81-208-4156-7

Also available at
MOTILAL BANARSIDASS
41 U.A., Bungalow Road, Jawahar Nagar, Delhi 110 007
1 B, Jyoti Studio Compound, Kennedy Bridge, Nana Chowk, Mumbai 400 007
203 Royapettah High Road, Mylapore, Chennai 600 004
236, 9th Main III Block, Jayanagar, Bangalore 560 011
8 Camac Street, Kolkata 700 017
Ashok Rajpath, Patna 800 004
Chowk, Varanasi 221 001

MLBD Cataloging-in-Publication Data
Vedic Concept of Dharma : A Philosophical Analysis
Original Oḍiā by DR. GANESWAR MISRA and
English Rendering by JAGANNATH DASH
ISBN : 978-81-208-4156-7
I. Hinduism II. Vedic Dharma
III. Philosophy IV.Misra, Ganeswar
V. Dash Jagannath

Published by
MOTILAL BANARSIDASS PUBLISHERS PRIVATE LIMITED
www.mlbd.com • mlbd@mlbd.com
Printed by Ajanta Offset and Packaging Limited

CONTENTS

Acknowledgement

This book 'Religion[1] of the Vedic Age' in *Oḍiā* language was prepared between March and December 1984, during which I was a Senior Fellow of the Indian Council of Philosophical Research.

Ganeswar Misra

---

1 Translator's Note: In the absence of an English word for the Saṁskṛt word 'Dharma', the author seems to have used the word 'Religion' here. The former word, however, is now included in the Addenda to The Oxford Universal Dictionary, 1976.

Translator's Acknowledgements and Comments

This book in *Oḍiā,* under the title *'Vaidika dharma-cetanā, eka dārśanika vicāra',* was dictated by my revered teacher and mentor, Professor Dr. Ganeswar Misra, after a close study of the Vedas in original, towards the ripest part of his mortal life. But the truth and enlightenment embodied in the book is immortal. The Vedas are not only secular of any Creator God or of any physical creation of the world, they are secular of any geographical, historical or locational limit. The Vedic sages are always universal in their thought, true of any part of the universe, and of the whole of the human society. I am grateful to my close friend and classmate Professor Dr. Bijayananda Kar who encouraged me to render the book into English. I am also thankful to Mr. Manorajnan Misra, Professor Dr. Ganeswar Misra's eldest son, who had earlier gifted a copy of the *Oḍiā* book to my wife and me.

I must clarify at the outset that I have attempted to rectify certain printing errors in the original *Oḍiā* text. I have also attempted to avoid some repetitions there. I have shifted the author's footnotes to near the related text for better appreciation. I have rendered certain words, such as *'devatā'* into 'dignitary', 'luminary', etc., and *'ātmā'* into 'awareness', 'simple-awareness', etc., consistently with the author's views that the Vedas are all about knowledge, linguistic usage and consequent human welfare (Ch.III), and that a *devatā* is not a theistic supernatural entity and *ātmā* is not a disembodied spirit (Ch.IV). Consistently with the author's overall approach I have added certain notes at appropriate places, mostly taking help of V.S. Apte's Saṁskṛt-English Dictionary and Ācārya Śaṅkara's and Muni Vidyāraṇya's commentaries.

Finally, I am grateful to my son, Professor Dr. Debiprasad Dash (Editor, *Journal of Research Practice*), for his meticulous assistance in proofreading the translation.

Jagannath Dash
84, Hatiasuni Lane
Bhubaneswar 751014, India

30 December 2016

In Brief (*Granthapraveśa*)

Even as a child I had developed an interest in the Vedas. Melodious and enchanting chantings of Vedic mantras such as 'Aum the breezes breath honey of propriety and order, the rivers flow honey ...' etc., in ceremonies of marriage, sacred thread and others, had caused a deep interest in my mind to know more about these. During my school days, Mahatma Gandhi, the Father of the Nation was creating a national awareness against the practice of untouchability then prevailing in the Hindu society. He was repeatedly warning that it was a societal stigma to keep a section, the śūdras[1] as untouchable. I was following his arguments from the paper 'Harijan'. I was convinced that his arguments were cogent. But on the other hand religious fanatics were not tired of quoting from the Gītā to uphold that God himself has created four castes, brāhmaṇa, kṣatriya, vaiśya and śūdra in keeping with their respective aptitudes and functions. But I could not see, from the relative verse of the Gītā, any justification for a permanent isolation of a section of the society. Further, some pundits, who knew the Vedas, argued that according to the Vedic 'Verse to the Person' śūdra was born from the feet of the primeval Person and was

1 Translator's Note: This word is interpreted by Śaṅkara as 'one overtaken by grief on hearing some disparaging remark on oneself'. Such a person is incapable of logical and linguistic analysis. "The conventional meaning (of the word) is inadmissible (B.S.1.3.34.)" in the context of a discourse on logical and linguistic analysis.

intended to serve the three remaining castes and therefore formed the lowest caste. Consequently, continued the pundits, it is clearly indicated in the Vedas that the śūdras are untouchable due to their low caste by birth. In the circumstances I was eager to myself peruse the Vedas. Initially I felt I needed someone to help me in this. I attended some discourses by some pundits on the Vedas, to find that their views and interpretations were far from convincing. But I was also hesitant if I could myself understand and fully appreciate the Vedic mantras couched in unusual expressions.

However, when I was invited by the Indian Council of Philosophical Research to submit a paper on 'Vedic Values and Approach to Life' for a seminar during March 1984, I resolved to read the Vedas myself. On reading 'The Verse of Knowledge', 'The Verse to the Person', 'Firm be my resolve', of the Ṛgveda, I was astonished to find myself at an entirely new view of the Vedas. I then went through 'The Song to the Soil' of the Atharva Veda. I was further encouraged to study 'The Verse to the śūdra and to Agronomy' of the Ṛgveda. Gradually I covered most of the Ṛgveda and gained a clear insight. The new insight was astounding to myself. The appropriate implications of the Vedas, distinct from the conventional interpretations were found to focus a fresh flood-light on the foundational truth. The more I read the more I was encouraged to read. Vedic dharma, I found, was the oldest of, and was clearly distinct from, all the religions of the world.

Before one can work towards the Good in life one needs to have clear knowledge about what is Good and what is Evil. Thus the first question that the noble sage tried to tackle was 'what are the distinctive nature and methods of knowledge?' An effective method of learning is to enquire and to seek clarifications from the learned. It was therefore logical for Ṛgveda to commence with many queries such as 'Who is this dignitary?', 'Why should one worship him?' etc. It became clear to me that all the Vedic mantras are designed as logical answers to such questions. The word 'Veda' means 'knowledge'. That is why Vedas are said to be founded on knowledge.

Knowledge depends on language but for which it cannot be placed in a presentable form. Unless it is presentable for independent analysis and scrutiny by many others, it is blind belief. Unless all participants adopt the same name for one thing, there cannot be any communication. There is no private language and no private knowledge. This is clearly pronounced in the Ṛgveda. Moreover, knowledge can be preserved for the progeny only as expressed in language, leading to the evolution of educational institutions of students and teachers. The participants in these institutions are called Brāhmaṇas.

Education facilitates a wholesome development. Education is a social institution. It gets designed, strengthened and developed through language. While language is created by the society, it subsequently works as a societal force of cohesion by facilitating exchange of ideas contributing to social organization, strength and friendship. Language owes its origin to the untiring efforts of the sages to name the nameless. That is why they are the pioneers, the progressive legislators of the whole of the human society. It is often pronounced in the Vedas, Ṛk through Atharva, that humanity owes its evolution to these sages. The Vedic sages are the seers of the mantras. The sage pioneered the path of analysis by presenting in language, for analytical scrutiny by wise men, in seminars, the truth he saw through deep concentration of mind. On such analytical scrutiny the truth that passes the test is expressed in sweet and melodious verse. Since the truth is the outcome of deep concentration of mind it is called a mantra and its author, the seer of the mantra. 'Seer' and 'vision' mean here 'what is known' or 'knowledge'. The sage does not say that he saw what was already expressed by someone else. The word '*darśana*' is used in the *śāstras* in this sense. In this sense Indian 'philosophical' knowledge is '*darśana*'. The Vedas are thus authored by the sages. The Vedas are neither auto-born nor are these promulgated by God. These are authored by men, but as their truths are independent of any individual's perception, and are in accordance with the nature of the percept, these mantras are called 'person-neutral'. Each mantra of the person-neutral Vedas is authored by one or the other of the sages. The Vedas do not recognize any individual's primacy. No one, neither the God, nor the Creator, nor a great man deputed by Him, has pronounced the Vedas.

There is no ordainment here. It is clearly recorded in the Vedas that these are authored by seven sages, Bhṛgu etc., and their progenies and that the Vedic dharma is rooted on the firm foundation of knowledge, that is 'truth' after analytical scrutiny by many wise men. Elsewhere, religious ordinances are inscrutable and are, therefore, dogmatic. As Vedic dharma is founded on knowledge and as knowledge is a social institution, it functions with contributions of many individuals, none of whom is indispensable.

Ordinances of other religions have no scope for epistemological questions whereas Vedic dharma is all about quests and about knowledge. Vedic mantras are not dogmatic assertions. These are about logical entities and are supported by logical arguments.

Another notable aspect of the Vedic dharma is that it has no place for a creator of the world. Vedas propound no theory of creation. It is rather with a scientific outlook that they conceive of an evolutionary process of gradual progress. It is but natural that knowledge displays a scientific thought. Basic existence is the root of all ramifications, says the Vedic sage. The world evolves out of a golden brilliance of possibilities. The axiomatic first principle is that 'existence is the golden womb that bears all brilliant possibilities, (*hiraṇya-garbhaḥ samavartata-agre*)'. This existence carried in its indiscrete heart, the sun, the moon, the stars, the sky, the space and the earth with its seas and soils as nameless entities. These became gradually discrete from out of this root. The named items of whatever is intelligible have gradually evolved out of the nameless. Initially bacteria bred in water and slowly evolved to aqua-bred and land-bred insects. In keeping with natural law, evolved the seasons, the spring, the summer, the showers that facilitates growth of grass, scrubs, trees and vegetations and then the bipeds, quadrupeds and finally, the homo sapiens. All this is a process of evolution. The men, through their language and knowledge, could trace out the concepts of order (*ṛta*) and truth (*satya*) etc., which again facilitated faster evolution, so that man leads all the other animals behind and wins the world.

Founded on knowledge, self-restraint, sense-control, steadiness, resoluteness and truth, human society shall ever evolve continuously, without a break. This unbroken continuity of the human society is the contribution of knowledge that dispels the deep darkness of ignorance (*āditya-varṇaṁ tamasaḥ parastāt*). Society is unbreakable, no individual is. The individual is the son of the unbroken (*amṛtasya putraḥ*) as a valid participant of the social enlightenment. Thus the goal of humanity is the achievement of a conscious awareness of this break-less, deathless societal continuity. An individual ought to invite death after living a fruitful life of hundred or 120 years. Yama is honorable having taught this truth. He was the first to emulate this truth and became the imitable dignified illustration of this principle of social welfare. Other dignitaries have similarly attained their status by establishing some such glorious illustrations of social welfare. Those who have obtained glory by substantially contributing to welfare of man are forever dignified in social memory. These illustrious persons are called 'dignitaries' (*devatā*). They are remembered as enlightening and brilliant examples. Vedas are eloquent in singing praises of their glory. One gets inspiration from these praising verses to conduct oneself along the desired path. Vedic mantras are eulogies, praises, not prayers. One gathers inestimable self-confidence, no inspiration for self-surrender at the feet of any Creator God, from participating in mere utterance of the names of these dignitaries in sacrificial congregations. On such occasions, animal instincts are sacrificed and one is consecrated into a second birth, a regeneration established in learning in sense-control and in self-constraint. One takes a second birth in accordance with the process of societal evolution. As knowledge and growth is possible only in a stable society, the Vedic mantra clearly visualizes that it is good for humanity as well as for an individual, that peace should prevail through interactive knowledge, orderly living, cooperative farming, fostering natural environment and through organized action to eliminate the countervailing forces. The approach of the Veda-dharma is towards a healthy and effective living free from wants and poverty and towards a life of affluence facilitated by group efforts. Veda-dharma and culture is all about an intellectually enlightened social humanism. There is no place for a Creator God and for one's servile self-surrender to Him.

Now the question is who, then, is this 'Person' with a thousand heads, eyes, hands and feet, of 'The Verse to the Person', if no creator is admitted? It is the enlightened inspired, cultured, ever-evolving 'Humanity' or 'Human Society'. This enlightened entity, with many individuals living together, inspired with a converging concern towards the gradual process of evolving unfoldment, has many brains and sense and motor organs. Occupational classifications evolved along with specialized knowledge and skill, within the society. Students and teachers are brāhmaṇas, engaged in knowledge-research. To implement their guidance for social well-being and to resolutely defend the civilized society from external aggression was the role of the kṣatriya, at the cost of his life. Similarly, the economic interest of the society is protected by the educated and aware economists, vaiśyas. There are also wage earners from manual work, śūdras. These classes arise from perceived distinctions in the social mind. Each of these classes is also a societal person. The whole of the society is the 'Prime-person'. The occupational classes are 'Other-persons' within the Prime-person. The Verse to the Śūdra and to Agronomy, Ṛk.4-57, p.99, and The Ode to Harvesting, Atharva 3.24, p.100, describe the organized farmers as the 'Field-person' who attend to their duties with attention and steadiness with their thousand heads, hands and eyes. The 'Person' in 'The Verse to the Person' is thus, not a Creator God.

One more word and I conclude. The concept of awareness (*ātman*) discussed in the Vedas is not that of a disembodied spirit. It is the human discriminating faculty (*viveka*) organized in order (*ṛta*) and truth (*satya*) capable of discriminating between what is good for man and what is not. This faculty was blunt in the primitive homo sapiens. It does not roam around as a disembodied spirit after the end of the body. This 'awareness' is the gift to us by Indra who brought into sharp focus the use of the concept organized in order and truth. He is thus the source of awareness. He is praised accordingly. He is also the source of strength (*vala*). The word 'awareness' was also used in this sense in the Rāmāyaṇa of Vālmikī. He talks of Rāma as an aware person (*ātmavān*). Awareness is earned even as one earns wealth. Awareness of good and of not-good is deathless even as the evolving society is. An individual's auto-awareness terminates at the termination of one's body. The glorious dignitaries (*devatā*) are deathless in social memory. An individual person is not deathless. His awareness along with his discriminating faculty terminates. As this unique Veda-dharma is founded entirely on truth and order, and as such, is acceptable to all men at all times, it is timeless. These are the topics discussed in more detail in the ensuing chapters.

134, Sahidnagar
Bhubaneswar

Ganeswar Misra

Chapter I

Concept of Dharma During the Vedic Age

The word 'dharma' is used in the post-Vedic *purāṇas* and in later literature to mean things entirely different from those of the Vedas. This new usage of the word is more or less similar to the concept of 'religion' prevalent in Europe and Asia. In this new usage 'religion' accommodates many tales and narratives concerning The Creator, theories of creation and dissolution and craving the Creator's grace etc. The dominant approach here is faith in God and surrender to Him. It is the sacrosanct faith that a sacred living ensures achievement of the ultimate target of life. In the *purāṇas* and in the various regional cultures of the world this ultimate target is described almost uniformly such as salvation, deliverance, gaining the greatest status, dissolution in God, joining God or a life with Him in the Heaven enjoying the greatest pleasure along with Him etc. Buddism calls it extinction (*nirvāṇa*). In Hinduism the *purāṇas* call it liberation (*mokṣa*). Extinction means cessation of sorrow. Sorrow owes to want. There are also many unavoidable sources such as old-age, death and disease etc., that cause sorrow. One can eliminate sorrow and can escape birth and death by extinguishing one's wants through religious living. According to *Mīmāṁsā* one earns virtue (*puṇya*) from a clean life lived on the lines of the prescribed code. This virtue ensures a residence in the

Heaven. The Heaven provides full opportunity for enjoyment of continuous pleasure. An opposite life leads to a residence in the Hell, full of sorrow and suffering. One returns to this world for a new body and life when vice and virtue are exhausted. According to the Bhāgavata, one gains a great position at the feet of the Creator Lord on continuous muttering (*japa*) of His name with devotion (*bhakti*) and penance (*tapasyā*). Thereafter one does not come back to this world of body and life full of sensual bewitchment leading to limitless sorrow and suffering. The ultimate target is described, more or less, on similar lines in Islam and Christian religions. One goes to the Lord by living a life along the path shown by the Great Mohammed deputed by The Allah. Similarly, one earns virtue through a life along the path shown by The Christ leading to God's Heaven of boundless bliss. Otherwise one earns sin and is accordingly condemned by God to appropriate Hell of suffering.

It is evident from the foregoing that these religions treat awareness (*ātman*) as a deathless bodyless spirit or soul. It goes to either Heaven or Hell after the end of the body or adopts a new body to live a lower or higher life in accordance with its vice or virtue earned earlier. The remarkable feature of these religions is that these have been taught by certain identified historical individuals. These individuals may be God himself or His son or messenger. Christianism was taught by Jesus Christ in the first century B.C. Islam was taught by Prophet Mohammed in the sixth century A.D. Jesus is

God's son. He teaches what God had told him and asks people to lead their lives accordingly. Prophet Mohammed is not God's son but was his messenger. He teaches what he learnt directly from Allah. Zoroaster teaches the Lord's (*Ahuramazda's*) words. Chaitanyaism is taught by Lord Śrī Chaitanya. Sectarian religions like *Śaiva, Vaiṣṇava, Śākta, Gāṇapatya, Saura* etc., worship an identified God and have been inspired by either these Gods or the persons selected by them. These religions are named after these Gods or their respective teachers. These religions discuss in detail about the Creator, theory of creation, target of life and appropriate rules and procedures of rituals. Any deviation is penalized. There is no scope for argument, logic, analysis or debate. No one is free to raise any question or to apply any analytical discrimination. What is important here is religious faith with complete subordination and surrender of intellect. Adam and Eve ate the tasty apple of knowledge and earned the wholesale condemnation of their progeny, the human race. In Hinduism God comes through faith and goes away through logic. Doubt and you are doomed. Unswerved faith is the root source of all these religions. Systems and procedures of marriage, rituals, prayers etc., are all designed according to divine desire. One has to serve the husband and rear the child according to God's will. In none of these areas there is any scope for intellectual analysis. What is important is unconsidered adoption of and devout subordination to the divine desire. One is bound to follow God's words and the relative systems and procedures. There can be no exception to or deviation from these dogmatic assertions. It is fundamental that one must have deep devotion to God and has to devoutly crave His grace so that one can strive to achieve the ultimate target of life through self-surrender and sacrifice. Only when there is some doubt in understanding the meaning of God's words one may consult a contemporary established commentator. There is no scope for any difference of opinion otherwise. Relying on interpretative subtleties sects can come into being. But intellectual light shall not be allowed to give rise to any difference of opinion.

Mysticism is another remarkable feature of all these religions. The Creator wills and astonishing effects accrue. Virgin Mary gives birth to God's son Jesus. A virgin cannot be a mother before contacting a male. Out of the blue there was an astounding light in the sky and simultaneously there was unprecedented delight, throb, pleasure and activeness in Mary's body. A bodyless voice was heard, 'Don't worry, God's son has entered your womb and will be born in right time to spread an unprecedented religion following which all men will have an opportunity to rise to the Heaven'. This account of birth is mystical. It happens only on God's will. Similar mystical events have been described in the *purāṇas* and thereafter. Eating of sacrificial oblation must effect pregnancy without any contact between a male and a female. Even a male will conceive eating this. King Yuvanāsva accidentally drank the consecrated water on the sacrificial altar and conceived the famous king Māndhātā. A man cannot deliver in the normal manner. So Māndhātā came out by tearing a path through the chest bones of his father. Virgin Kunti became pregnant by simply thinking of Dharmarāja (Translator's Note: It was the Sun God, *vide.,* V.S. Apte) and the child was born through her ear. So he was the Earboy (Karṇa). What God wills shall happen, be it possible or impossible. 'The dumb can be talkative, the lame can jump over a hill, I salute thee O' *Paramānandamādhava*, your grace grants everything'. All these are mystical. Doubt this and you are doomed. Unquestioned faith in all these leads one to Heaven. Question this and one goes to Hell.

All religions believe in the wishful Creator God. He is omnipotent and can bring about all sorts of amazing events. He is also a magician (*māyāvī*). His magic is unintelligible. It is simple haughtiness to try to understand this. Whatever He has said or has made to be said must be accepted. Doubt inspired by intellectual analysis (*vicāra*) leads one straight to Hell. One earns virtue by believing all this word by word. There can be no divergence from the words and directives of God. These dogmas are far away from intellect, analysis or logic. It is sin to try to apply analysis or knowledge. Keep aside knowledge, have absolute devotion and faith, obey and abide by. In the words of the devotee poet Madhusūdana, 'placed at the bottom, I am Thy child, impotent and ignorant (*adhama akṣama avodha vāḷaka*)'.

There is no trace of any of such ideas in the Vedas. The Vedas ask us to try to committedly abide by certain universal norms and patterns that will contribute to social stability and to the welfare of the whole of the humanity. These norms and patterns are the outcome of deep deliberations of the sages and have been finalized through discussion and debating by many wise men. Since the resolute observance of these contributes to social stability, the relative conduct is dharma. That which holds the society firmly together as well as facilitates social welfare is dharma (*dhriyate* or *dhāraṇāt dharma*). This knowledge-based and welfare-facilitating feature of Veda-dharma is discussed in greater detail in the next chapter.

Veda-dharma knows no Creator, no theory of creation. It talks of no mysterious outcome. It accords no singular pre-eminence to any particular individual. It is founded on truth realized by different members of seven different families at various points of time. The views of these individuals, moreover, evolved as stable social conducts only after these were thoroughly deliberated and debated upon by several wise men in many conferences and seminars. Ṛgveda states explicitly that the world to which common men as well as dignitaries (*devatā*) are born was already governed by order (*ṛta*). These dignitaries of the Vedas are facilitators of common good and welfare. They are therefore glorious. Our glorious predecessors (*pitṛ*) are also brilliant lights in social memory and beacon us along the right social path. The word *'devatā'* (lit., a shining dignitary, often inaccurately translated as 'God') comes from the root '*div*' (to shine). Indra in the *Saṁhitā* age leads the war against the sensuous (*asura*) to defend the sensible (*ārya*) invisibly, even as Lord Jagannātha is said to have invisibly led the war against Kāñci. Since ethical and social order was initiated by these enlightened dignitaries they are described as creators of human society or of social humanity. As Manu has codified these orders men are forever indebted to him and are accordingly designated as men (*mānava* = of Manu). An individual cannot be immortal but can live long enough to succeed in his endeavours. It is only the society, its sense of value and its ethical order that are enduring and perpetual. The enlightened dignitary Yama teaches us to live an effective life and to be ready to welcome death when the body becomes terminally tired. Youthful boys and girls of the Vedic age are said to have digested poison because they have successfully completed their education while residing in the hermitages of the sages in very stern and stringent discipline of ethics and self-constraint. They are like Yama thus prepared to sacrifice their lives to defend the culture. Thus seasoned they return home after the convocation. They defend even the dignitaries, i.e., they come forward to defend social stability envisaged by the dignitaries. Marriage is according to the choice of boys and girls. Women are as much educated and wise as men. Many Vedic mantras are authored by women. We will have occasion to discuss more on the point in the next chapter. The Person of

'The Verse to the Person' is only the aware societal humanity. None of the four professional classes talked of in the Vedas are 'upper' or 'lower', all are upheld as useful social segments. While enumerating these classes the name śūdra is stated before vaiśya at times. Since śūdras are specialized in agricultural skills they are upheld as the 'Field Person' (*Kṣetra-Puruṣa*). The Person with a hundred hands means a group of fifty persons engaged in agricultural activities. They are also described as a hundred handed person because the group works together with a single commitment to their work. Similarly, where thousands of persons work together they are called as a thousand headed person as a group. From the harvest, nine parts out of sixteen, is prescribed as their rightful due in recognition of their expertise. This will be explained in more detail in Chapter V, 'The Verse to the Person'. No one among the dignitaries mentioned in the Vedas is more or less important. Each one is a pioneer in guiding the evolution of social culture and is therefore equally praiseworthy.

As the Vedas are founded on truth and are therefore acceptable to all, there is no scope for any divine ordainment. Vedas derive from truth and knowledge and from no commandment. It follows that there is no scope for religious conversion. The Vedas exhort all to relentlessly pursue the path of truth. Truth is one, not many. Thus there can be no issue at all of many dharmas. Vedadharma is valid at all times for all individuals (*sanātana*). Truth is independent of any individual person. It is not that a rich man tells the truth and the poor otherwise. Truth is factual (*vastutantra*) and impersonal. Whether a statement is true or otherwise depends not at all on who has authored it, but on whether or not it states facts and events as they occur. In this view the Vedas are impersonal (*apauruṣeya*). Religious commandments, on the other hand, are mandatory and inviolable because these are enjoined by great men and God-men.

'One male to marry one female', is a pragmatically sound system, says the Ṛgveda. It does justice to both the partners even though it is not a sacrosanct command of any God or God-man. Ṛgveda also says that a young female should marry again instead of life-long grieving and lamenting the untimely death of her husband. One should not gamble lest he loses everything and becomes a pauper to the utter misfortune of his dependants. Gambling is unacceptable to a logical mind. This will come up for discussion in the next chapter.

Chapter II

Vedic Dharma is Distinct From Religions of Later Ages

Veda-dharma accords no primacy to any Great Person. It has not been taught by any Great Man at any point of time. No single sage is the author of all the mantras. Seven sages and their progenies have authored the mantras over a long period of time spreading over many years. Angīrasa, his son Bṛhaspati, his son Bharadvāja and their progenies such as Śiśu, Bhikṣu and Saṁvanana have authored many mantras. Viśvāmitra is the son of Gādhi. Prajāpati and Madhuchanda are Viśvāmitra's sons. Aghamarṣaṇa and Ucathya are Madhuchanda's sons. Dīrghatamas is the son of Ucathya. Each of them has authored many mantras. The said seven sages are Bhṛgu, Viśvāmitra, Gautama, Atri, Bharadvāja, Vaśiṣṭha and Kaśyapa. No surprise that many wise women of this age, such as Ghoṣā, Apālā, Indrāṇī, Śacī Paulomī etc., have also authored many mantras. Ghoṣā authors two verses of the Ṛgveda (10.39). In one she declares that 'this eulogy is as dear to me as the bride is to the groom'. In the second one she prays the two Aśvinīs, saying, 'A princess, I pray thee'. Similarly, Apālā describes herself a virgin who met the Soma on her way to the river to fetch water. Indrāṇi in her eulogy exhorts her husband 'to be loyal to her alone'. Śacī Paulomī declares 'My husband is loyal to me as a conquered is to the conqueror'. These poetesses have authored eulogies concerning love and conjugal life. We will have occasion to discuss later (Ch.VII) how pervasive was womens' education at least 6,000 years back.

Vedic sages are said to be 'seers of mantras'. 'Mantra' is the truth realized from deep concentration of mind. 'Seer' means the 'knower' in general and not merely the visual percipient. It covers all sense perceptions as well as mental and intellectual awareness. Though the word 'viśion' (*darśana*) literally comes from the root 'to see' (*dṛś*), philosophically it covers knowledge from all sense organs as well as from mind (*mana*) and intellect (*buddhi*). Thus, a 'seer of mantra' is one whose knowledge that beacons practical life towards a fruitful living, is the outcome of deep meditation, and has been authenticated or validated after astute audit and intense debating by many wise men. A 'seer' who is the visionary of universal good, is no Creator God.

The sage expresses the mantra that he sees which is later formulated as a eulogy, after it passes due scrutiny and debating by many wise-men. Thus the sage is also accredited as the author of such eulogical hymns.

One ought to be clear that the Vedas have later been described as 'impersonal' (*apauruṣeya*). It does not mean that these have no human author. Ācārya Śaṅkara states that every Vedic eulogy or mantra states its own author.[1] One tends to laugh at the statement that 'the Vedas have no author'. The name of its author is clearly stated with every obeisance, eulogy, benediction and verse. There is no *sūkta* not preceded by the name of its author. It is therefore, entirely absurd to say that the Vedas have no human author.

Ācārya Śaṅkara provides the clue to the meaning of the word 'impersonal'. The mantras express eternal truth. Truth is not an effect of any causal manipulation by any person (*puruṣa-vyāpāra-tantraṁ*). It occurs all by itself in accordance with the nature of the object (*vastu-tantraṁ*) of knowledge and the method of knowledge (*pramāṇa-janyaṁ*)[2]. Truth of a statement owes nothing to the greatness of the seer and maker thereof. It is accorded the status of truth if it conforms to the thing talked of.

The sages are not only seers of truth but are also poets of the mantras, eulogies, etc. The elegant, ornamental and accurate expressions of the Vedic literature establish that they are poems as well. The linguistic expressions employed are eminently appropriate to the depth of the mantras. The tenth Chapter (*maṇḍala*) of the Ṛgveda describes the sages as

---

[1] Translator's Note: "The Vedas also show that the rites are to be performed with mantras after knowing their seers," BSSB, 1.3.30, Gambhirananda, 4th edition, 1983, p. 219, Line 21.

[2] Translator's Note: "The knowledge of Brahman is not dependent on human action.... It is dependent on the thing itself, as in the case of the knowledge of a thing got through such valid means as direct perception", BSSB, 1.1.4, Gambhirananda, 4th edition, 1983, p. 30, Lines 20 to 25.

pioneers in coining new linguistic expressions. They discovered the capacity of language to communicate. The Ṛgveda terms this capacity as 'The Great Master' (*Bṛhaspati*) at No.10.71. The collaborative efforts of these poets to express meaning through elegant and appropriate language is eulogized here in the following words. 'The sages observed utmost caution, while interacting in group discussions to coin words for ideas, even as one does while screening out fine flour free of any coarseness'. Their language is thus accurate to express the acute meanings of the mantras. Knowledge cannot occur without language. Language is the only essential medium of communication and scrutiny of knowledge. Language is the body of knowledge. Knowledge cannot be formulated without language. Mere awareness (*ātmā*) is inarticulate without a linguistic body. I know something. I communicate it to others through language. They are thus enabled to analyse and scrutinize my knowledge so that it is found to be validated or otherwise. Knowledge is not a flash of light but a mere screen of fog if there is no scope for its public scrutiny in the absence of its linguistic communication. The hymn indicates this feature of language and knowledge while contending that one should be able to distinguish what encourages from what discourages social progress. There is no knowledge without language that is founded on and that grows out of the need alone of a communicative community. Progress in any field owes essentially to a social context. An organized society is the foundation of all progress. Knowledge is latent at the time of birth of a child as also in a primitive society. It gets expression later. Knowledge sublates disintegration (*mṛtyu*). We will revert to this concept in the Verse to the Person (Ch.V), in the context of societal personality. The succeeding brilliant light of knowledge evolves out of a preceding darkness of nescience, i.e., *ādityavarṇaṁ tamasaḥ parastāt*. Thus the seers are also poets. They have designed expressive language to present the subtle meanings of the mantras. Their language is expressive as well as melodious and thought-provoking. They are also similarly described as *yaritri* (a singer), *kārīn* (a builder), *kāru* (an architect of words), *takṣa* (a carpenter), *vipra* (an aware person), *dhīra* (intelligent), *manīṣī* (of sharp intellect) and *vedhas* (wise) etc. They are very highly accomplished creators of new linguistic expressions. They are the founding fathers and prime movers of societal culture. They have laid down the initial guidelines for progress towards truth, ethics and knowledge. These guidelines are enshrined in musical songs, suitable for melodious chanting. They have asked us to sing in praise, the eulogies of those brilliant dignitaries who have laid down their lives to protect and to preserve humanity and its culture, with unprecedented courage, perseverance, heroism and prowess. These melodious eulogies keep on constantly reminding us of the glory of the dignitaries (*devatā*) who ought to be ever close (*upāsya*) to our hearts on account of their singular services towards growth of human culture. The word 'dignitary' means 'a brilliant light', an enlightened person. In answer to the questions concerning these dignitaries Ṛgveda is never tired of singing eulogies of their relentless brilliant performances. Virtue consists in observing the rules of conduct that contribute to realizing in the life, what is considered to be of enduring value. Any infraction of this is vice, declare the Vedas. The Veda (knowledge) is a collection of poems concerning the nature of knowledge. It therefore eulogises speech (*Sarasvatī*), the symbol of knowledge. The Vedas are also called 'a collection of eulogies', i.e., *Saṁhitā*.

Veda-dharma is thus founded on knowledge. It does not discourage knowledge. It believes in no pre-eminence of any individual and of any Great Man. Veda-dharma recognizes no ordainment of any Great Man saying, 'Do as I command, so you will go to God in the Heaven of durable pleasure, there is no alternative'. No command, no statement will be acceptable except after elaborate analytical scrutiny (*vicāra*). Veda-dharma is all about rational knowledge. It talks neither of supernatural spirits (*adhyātmavāda*) nor of external physical objects (*bhautikavāda*). It can be depicted as 'humanism'. Its dominant perspective is human welfare. The book, that strings together such truths as are likely to contribute to growth of human good, is Veda, i.e., rational knowledge and no dogmatism.

Founded on truth, Veda-dharma is *'sanātana'*, i.e., a-temporal and is valid for all individuals at all times. Having been developed and practised in the cultured (*ārya*) society it is the cultured dharma (*āryadharma*). Those who came in from west, initially saw it prevailing in the valley of the river Sindhu (Indus) and incidentally came to call it Hindu dharma. There is no founder of the Veda-dharma. No Great Man descended from the Heavens to this mundane earth at any point of time in history to found or propound this Veda-dharma. Unlike in later religions no one ordains here, 'Obey me to earn virtue and to meet God or disobey me and go to Hell'. No one claims here to be The God Himself or His only trusted Deputy or His single beloved Messenger or the only Great Man entitled to pronounce God's words. There is no scope at all in this Veda-dharma for any dogmatic adherence to any great man's words. There is no ordainment here accepted without analytical critique. Truth and knowledge alone is its foundation. Only those truths can contribute to social welfare, which have emerged from the collaborative efforts of many wise and learned persons offering thread-bare analysis in many seminars and conferences during the *Saṁhitā* age. An individual's welfare is derived from social welfare. These true statements are said to be the order (*ṛta*) of a purposeful life. Even today some of the Vedic mantras are chanted in social congregations and auspicious occasions. Since knowledge and truth are independent of any individual's psychological perception, Veda-dharma knows no personal pre-eminence at all.

It is 'truth' that facilitates societal well-being. These truths have been detailed by the seers only after these were subjected to rigorous meditation of and detailed debating by many participants. Such debating commands deep wisdom (*prajñā*) and understanding (*dhī*). The truth that comes to light through the focus of such aware wisdom is 'knowledge'. As the Vedas are replete with detailed discussions about truth accomplished by knowledge, we will discuss the Vedic views about the methods and features of knowledge in the next chapter. Later religions allow no scope for debating and consequently no scope for raising questions in case of doubt. But Veda-dharma provides for full scope for raising questions. It asks one to accept anything only after detailed analysis and scrutiny. The questions that are answered by the Veda-mantras will also be discussed in detail in the following pages. It has been realized as a basic requisite that one ought to raise questions in Vedic debating. Raising questions is seen as the method that leads to knowledge. It was clearly recognized that one must ask appropriate questions to elicit relevant answers before one can achieve clarity of knowledge. This recognition is embodied in a subsequent upaniṣad named 'Question' (Praśna). With a view to distinguish between questions that are genuine ones and those that are meaningless, Gārgī has been projected as a standard questioner

(Br.Up.Ch.3). I wish to discuss this and other issues in more detail on the upaniṣads later.[1]

All the life-elevating truths, brought to light by the seers, were found by them to have been rooted in one's conscious resolve (*śiva-saṅkalpa*) to aim at societal well-being, i.e., universal good. This is recorded in the **'Verse of Conscious Resolve for Universal Good'**. A literal rendering of the verse follows.

Yajurveda, Ch. 34

'My mind can transcend all its states, waking to deep sleep. It is the light of all lights. Let that, my mind, consciously resolve for universal good' (*tat me manaḥ śivasaṅkalpaṁ astu*).

'It impels wise-men to sacrifice. It facilitates, through intellect, incisive analysis for truth. It is the matchless brilliance immanent in all. Let that, my mind, consciously resolve for universal Good.'

'It sustains depth of knowledge, intellect and memory. It is the break-less-flame (*amṛta-śikhā*) of effulgence in all. Ignore it, and no one can do anything. Let that, my mind, consciously resolve for universal good.'

'It is break-less (*amṛta*). It unfolds the past, the present and the future. Its brilliance enables the seven priests to expand sacrifices. Let that, my mind, consciously resolve for universal good'.

---

1 Translator's Note: This did not materialize.

'The Ṛk, Sāma and Yajuṣ, Vedas are coherently held in place by the mind, even as the spokes are firmly held together by the nave. Let that, my mind, consciously resolve for universal good'.

'The mind guides the racing horses along the desired course. That dynamic and ever-active mind resides in the hearts of men. Let that, my mind, consciously resolve for universal good'.

Similarly, the verse **'May it all go on well' (*Svasti*)** wills as follows.

Ṛgveda, Sūkta 1.89

'Let noble thoughts flow in to us from all quarters, fully, freely and unfettered; so the dignitaries will volunteer to lead us always along the path of progress, even as wardens do unto their wards'.

It is evident from these verses (*sūkta*, lit. well-said) that the sages have called upon the world to strive for the well-being of the whole of the human race. Not satisfied, they have gone ahead further to assert that the human mind is eminently suited for the purpose. It can distinguish between what is good and what is evil. It is also capable, like a charioteer, of leading one along the path of the good. What is needed is only a firm commitment to self-control, self-discipline and a conscientious approach, so that one shall pursue the path of the good and shall relentlessly avoid that of the evil. The sage holds that he asks us to consciously resolve to work for common good, because we are capable to do so. There is no point otherwise, in sermonizing one to do something beyond one's capability. We also learn from the sage that we must cultivate our minds to be prepared to receive such ideas as can lead humanity towards universal good; no matter who is the author of the idea. Far from seeing others as irreligious, degraded or anti-religious, the sage finds that all segments of human society are full of many valuable ideas worthy of emulation. He knows for certain that the foundation of an all-inclusive social progress derives from the openness of one's mind, far removed from a dogmatic closed religious cult.

It is not that the sage was fully preoccupied only with very high moral standards at all times. He was equally alive to one's conduct in the mundane day to day life. He identifies and asks us to scrupulously desist from certain weaknesses that often attract a common man. To gamble with a stake is one such common weakness. It leads to endless misfortune. The sage warns against the weakness. 'Do not gamble. Cultivate your land and happily enjoy the produce. O' gambler with a stake! Think once, you have cattle, you have a wife and a family. It occurs to me straight from dignified illumination (*savitṛ-deva*)', Ṛgveda, 10.34.13. Gambling with a stake can lead to one's loss of cattle and can turn one's dependants to beggars on the street. No one should be attracted to gambling. If one adopts some profitable profession like, say, agriculture, one derives honest happiness to enjoy its outcome. The urge to earn from stakes in gambling is an endless bewitchment.

The sage also holds that one earns friends by feeding the hungry and also by helping the poor. One who does not help the poor and the weak will have no sympathizer. For the sage, hunger is not a direct and natural cause of death. One with enough food dies due to other causes. Death due to hunger is a stigmatic stain on the societal structure. It can surely be prevented. It is a sin to eat before feeding a hungry man. This is the point of Verse 117 of the 10th Manḍala of the Ṛgveda. Feed the hungry or go to hell. The point is not that God will be angry with you. The sage shows the reason why it is obligatory to feed the hungry. The mantra is no dogma. It is founded on knowledge and cogent logic.

The sages are ever memorable for all men as the architects of these universal guidelines. The dignitaries are glorious because they consult the sages concerning what is good for humanity. Thus it is the Veda-dharma that the God (dignitary) consults men (sages), and the former is, therefore, not the creator of the world (of men). The dignitaries are past or present participants in human progress. During life they are devoted to human welfare, interacting with and consulting wise men, and after death live forever in social memory.

The sage saw the truth through his deep concentration and intense meditation. But it is not counted as true of universal well-being unless and until it is fully debated upon in congregations of wise men and refined accordingly. Seen in this light the Vedas emphasize truth and not the seer or author thereof, because the truth embodied in a mantra is firmly founded on the collaborative contributions of many wise men, even though the truth is seen and the mantra is authored by a sage. Truth owes nothing to any one person who sees it. An individual as such, deserves no pre-eminence at all. Truth is independent of any action of an individual. Truth is true for ever. It may be interesting to historians to know which individual or which society came across the truth at which point of time. But this historical investigation contributes nothing to the validity of truth. Truth is time-neutral (*cirantana*). In this view of the matter the Vedas are a-personal (*apauruṣeya*) or public (*nirvyaktika*).

Chapter III

Knowledge: Its Methods and Features

In the preceding chapter we said that Veda-dharma knows neither any super-sensual knowledge (*atīndriya-vāda*) nor any super-natural spirit (*ādhyātmika-vāda*). It is humanist (*mānava-vādī*). Achievement of the greatest good of humanity is the highest objective (*parama-puruṣārtha*) of human life. This will be highlighted in the next chapter citing the relative Vedic mantras. But while working towards the good of humanity, one ought to have a clear knowledge about what is good and what is evil, lest one may either pursue evil in the name of good or one may prevent good instead of evil. The humanist Vedic culture thus very acutely realizes that knowledge is the single most important pre-requisite for social good. The Vedas therefore give a clarion call that one ought to constantly keep one's intellect, the instrument of knowledge, wide open and awake at all times. These are the two points that come out clearly from the mantras cited in this chapter. Many of the Ṛgvedic verses clearly and studiously bring out very relevant notions concerning the methods and features of knowledge.

Methods of Knowledge

One of the inescapable and widely accepted methods of knowledge is to raise appropriate queries.

The environment for pondering over an issue consists of raising various questions to work out alternative possibilities. Without this only dogmatic views will becloud the mind far from a clarity of epistemic light. One has to ask an appropriate question to a knowledgeable person and take the latter's reply seriously for studious exercise and application so that the method of knowledge becomes free from possible misapplications. This is the only means by which there will be progress towards dawning of knowledge. "One who is ignorant of the route in an unknown country seeks guidance from another who knows and studiously proceeds according to the latter's direction to reach the destination. This is the benefit from relying on the knower's advice. The ignorant comes to know the route and proceeds along", says sage Kavaṣa (Ṛk.10.32.7.). Yajurveda similarly announces (19.30) that studious application educates (*dīkṣā*). Education sharpens one's skill (*dakṣiṇā*). Skill facilitates confidence (*śraddhā*) towards the search for truth (*satya*) leading to realization thereof, the conclusion of education. In the same vein, in the context of seeking knowledge by asking questions, asks sage Dīrghatama, son of Ucathya (Ṛk.1.164.6.), "I seek from the knowledgeable sages the information about what is the universal bond that firmly holds together the world (*Jagat*=all that becomes) consisting of six layers such as the base (*bhūloka*), the limits (*svarga loka*) etc., I am not very clear on the point".

It is obvious from these mantras that since the Vedas are founded on knowledge, they provide for complete scope to raise genuine questions. The Vedic mantras coined in melodious, simple and ornamental language are answers to genuine questions raised by inquisitive seekers of Veda, knowledge. It is the Veda-dharma alone that encourages seekers to ask questions, unlike any other religion anywhere in the world. All religions command the common man to uncritically accept what the prophets have pronounced and to conduct accordingly. This is an important distinction of the Veda-dharma from all religions.

In the context, we now quote the following quests of sage Hiraṇyagarbha, son of Prajāpati, in Ṛgveda (10.121).

1. "It is the womb of all possibilities (*Hiraṇyagarbhaḥ*, the goldmine), the base (*pati*) that precedes (*agre*) whatever becomes (*jāta*), the one that firmly supports the whole world (*bhūta*); be it the earth or be it the heavens. Who is the dignitary that engulfs all the data (*habiḥ*=lit., oblation) in order (*kasmai devāya habiṣā vidhema*)?" The entire world of experience was implicit in the intellectual womb of brilliant possibilities before becoming explicit in knowledge.
2. "Who is the dignitary that bestows awareness (*ātmā*) and potency (*vala*)? Men and dignitaries are held in place with his blessings. Who is the dignitary that provides the context (*chāyā*) for disintegration (*mṛtyu*) and for breaklessness (*amaratva*)? Who is

the dignitary that engulfs all the data in order?" This is an enquiry about the dignitaries, Indra and Yama. Indra organizes order (*ṛta*), the source of the potentials of discriminating (*viveka*) awareness (*ātmā*). Yama is the sustainer of the concepts of disintegration and breaklessness, described as the one who was the first to invite death and to organize the 'Heavenly World' for the dignitaries and the 'World of the Manes' for our departed forefathers. This idea comes out more clearly at the appropriate place of The Verse To The Person (Ch.V).

3. "Who is the dignitary that graciously presides over all the live and aware bipeds and quadrupeds? Who is the dignitary that engulfs all the data in order?" The mantra is a quest about the live and conscious class of men. One who is capable of acquiring knowledge has to live with others so that communication of knowledge and of news can take place.
4. "Who is the dignitary said to hold the world together, with his graceful long arms extending everywhere, be it the snow-clad mountain peak, be it the river that glides or be it the vastness of the ocean? Who is the dignitary that engulfs all the data in order?" The idea is, men spread out everywhere in their inquisitive anxiety to know about every detail all-round. The sage says that men always strive to know every conceivable component of the world.

5. "Who is the dignitary that firmly holds the earth and the heavens together; that locates space and light; and that maps out the water-bearing clouds in the sky? Who is the dignitary that engulfs all the data in order?" The sun, the moon, the earth and the various locations and things on the earth and their distances etc., from each other, were worked out in knowledge by means of use of language, to cognize them by coining names for them as a result of collaborative interactions of men. The sun, the moon, the stars and the hills were identified by the roaming men to locate places, distances and directions etc.
6. "Who is it that accounts for the glorious powers of the mind and of the intellect? Who is it that both the heaven and the earth look upon for expression? The sun rises and shines bright alike on both of them. Who is the dignitary that engulfs all the data in order?" Men had collected relevant data concerning the clouds to predict the rains.
7. "When life gushed forth along with water and lighted the lamp of life, the dignitaries remained coordinated as if into a single life. Who is the dignitary that engulfs all the data in order?" Microbes germinate in water. These mutate into plants, animals and men suitable for life on land when water recedes. Although the dignitaries were initially identified on account of their specific contributions towards social good, the coordinated urge for universal well-being was always at the root.

8. "Who is the single dignitary of all dignitaries that scans, by virtue of its own infinite power, the vast flooded environment to effectively work out various sacrifices? Who is the dignitary that engulfs all the data in order?" Initially men scanned the environment and observed that light (knowledge) sacrifices (dispels) darkness (ignorance). Discovery of fire not only provided protection from cold weather, it also facilitated visibility to locate things and aggressors. It is only then that all subsequent developments gradually ensued.
9. "Who is the dignitary that fathers the world? He is non-violent. On the premise that truth was the only inviolable restraint he worked out the heaven as well as the vast beautiful ocean. Who is the dignitary that engulfs all the data in order?" Even the aborigine has reared up its progenies, protecting against violence so that humanity survives and prospers sustained by appropriate code of conduct worked out by Prajāpati. One who abides by the code is praised, and one who violates, is discouraged, the code was the very foundation of societal and moral well-being, says Prajāpati.
10. "Whatever is or comes to be there in the world, is permeated by you O! Prajāpati. Let the objectives of our sacrifices be fulfilled, let us be wealthy." Humanity survives abiding by the social and moral code of conduct because Prajāpati, i.e., the urge to abide by the social and moral code, permeates all men.

While the questions are raised in one place, the whole of the Ṛgveda is in answer to these quests. The timeless truths implied in the Veda owe to these questions and their appropriate solutions. The solutions offered by the various sages are the outcomes of their deep thinking (*manana*). The sages presented their realisations in debates of wise-men (*vidatha*). Whatever undisputed truth emerges from exhaustive debates and deliberations is then recorded in melodious poetic form in appropriate metres suitable for enchanting musical recitations. These are the mantras, the outcomes of deep thinking. While the sage who initially presented the thought is recognized as its author, it was refined, expanded and was given a clear and intelligible linguistic form as a result of these deep deliberations by all the wise men before it was finally approved and adopted. Thus the sages are also 'seers' and 'poets'. This series of quests culminates in a declaration of an agenda, "Let the objectives of our sacrifices be fulfilled, let us be wealthy". This constitutes the clear declaration of the Vedic humanist approach. The Vedic sage does not dismiss the world as full of grief, sorrow and sufferings, that therefore the world has to be renounced and that one's well-being consists in surrendering to the creator after renouncing His creation. The clear agenda of the sage emphatically exhorts, let us have, in abundance, whatever facilitates living in this world, with happiness, friendship and peace.

Features of Knowledge (The Verse of Knowledge, *jñānaśūkta)*

The idea of 'truth' as 'impersonal' and 'timeless', has come into focus in answer to the questions discussed above. But one may doubt whether this idea is knowledge proper. To dispel such doubt, one has to ascertain 'what are the features of knowledge', lest non-knowledge is taken as knowledge and knowledge mistaken as non-knowledge. To safeguard against such possible pitfalls Ṛgveda provides exhaustive opportunities to discuss the features of knowledge. The Veda lays down (Ṛk.10.71.1 to 11) the features of knowledge as follows. The seer of these verses is Bṛhaspati, a progeny of Angirasa.

1. "O' Bṛhaspati! The sages evolved language to name the nameless things. It was their unique and highest contribution towards clarity and transparency. The use of language was initially confined among the sages. With loving affection, they later taught others this enlightened and invaluable skill to use language".
2. "Engaged with rapt attention, in the process of working out linguistic expressions, the group of sages was very cautiously refining these expressions, even as one screens out fine flour free of any coarseness. They discovered that language was the bond of love and friendship. They clearly noticed that all the beauty and sweetness of the cohesive force of love and friendship was immanent in language".

3. "Step after step, negotiating the linguistic stairs in the lime-light of sacrifices, they finally reached the knowledge that blossomed in the bosom of the sage. Having thus acquired, they spread out the mantras in the public from place to place, a group of seven musicians singing the mantras in soothing and enchanting chorus".
4. "One sees things but ignores the linguistic sense. One listens to sounds but ignores the linguistic essence. But there are some for whom speech (*vāk-devī*), the heavenly damsel, displays her sublime beauty, embellished as never before, even as a loving wife does".
5. "There may be a person who is taken for granted as a firm friend, but is not invited to participate in debates and disputations in critical conferences. Such a person is like one who is aimlessly wandering in a vast desert, confounded, as it were, running after foggy phantoms. His language bears no flowers, no fruits".
6. "Enlightening language has no depth for a person who runs around hither and thither ignoring the wise, the real friend. This person is likely to misunderstand what he hears. It can be reliably said that such a person is ignorant of the path of beatitude and blessedness".
7. "Friends with normal sight and audition may have unequal intellect. While one may be like a narrow, shallow puddle, the other may be like a deep, wide

lake where any number of persons can find enough space to dive, swim and bathe".

8. "Awake to the urge of the heart and the head, when friends organize sacrifices chanting Veda-mantras, some who are inexperienced may follow the leaders who go ahead and get recognized as experts in Vedic knowledge".
9. "There may be some others who can neither follow nor go ahead with expertise. They lack knowledge and are incapable of organizing sacrifices. They are fools. They only superficially spread out the mantras having got the words by heart. They prolong the words of the mantras, even as a weaver externally unwinds his threads".
10. "But the friend who actively participates in conferences and seminars of wise-men, and displaying expertise in logic and debating, makes his point emphatic and wins the debate, is always welcomed by people who volunteer to provide for his wherewithal".
11. "One is capable of diving into the depth of the verse. Another is an expert in melodious chanting in metre *śakvarī* (a class of metres with 14 syllables in a quarter). One knows, interpretes and explains the implications of what the Veda says. The other one records the systems and procedures of sacrificial rituals".

To sum up, the first four mantras bring out that use of language is the necessary antecedent of knowledge. In the absence of language no one can ask any question, nor can anyone give any answer, to acquire or impart any knowledge. Whatever we determine in knowledge is possible only by means of application of linguistic expression. The things lying invisible underneath the muddy waters of the mental stream can come to sight only on being flushed out by the linguistic fishing net. It is only the words used in a sentence that account for clarity of thought which is otherwise vague and hazy. Thus the sages pronounced the names of various things and situations so that with the help of knowledge one can be conscious of what is good for life. They evolved language and taught it to others so that it can function as the conveyance for communication of knowledge. Thus language is a public instrument. Unless there is a convention to use one name for one thing no one can use the same word to convey the same meaning. As language is necessary for knowledge, and since language is a public instrument, it is clear that knowledge is a public entity. Unless I communicate my knowledge to others and unless others accept it after due consideration and scrutiny, what appears to me as my personal knowledge is no knowledge. I could have misperceived and/or misconceived. Whether my belief is knowledge will be confirmed only after it is critically studied, examined and confirmed by others. The fifth mantra, therefore, conceives of a person who believes he knows something all by himself, and having worked out, employs a private linguistic expression to delineate his belief. The belief of such a person is as enigmatic as, say, a mirage in a desert. His linguistic usage is like a baren plant that bears no flower or fruit. One who is not initiated into the linguistic community and is ignorant of the public nature of linguistic usage, can have no idea as to what to say and to whom, when there is no one else in one's psychic territory. The sixth mantra declares that the public character of linguistic conventions is to be learnt from the seniors in order to understand linguistic expressions, to acquire and to enjoy the beatitude and blessings of knowledge. The seventh mantra recognizes that different persons may have different levels of expertise in learning and using language. One may be an expert in expressing very subtle ideas. Others may not match. All may not be equally capable of coining appropriate linguistic expressions to analyse and explain involved and complex concepts. The eleventh mantra, thus, segregates a singer with appropriate intonation and pronunciation, a theorist with appropriate expression and a performer in keeping with appropriate systems and procedures, in accordance with their respective distinctive skills and expertise. These persons are to be employed, in sacrificial functions, to work in their own fields of expertise. The theorist, however, being better equipped to have an overall view of the whole scenario is to remain in charge of general management. The eighth and ninth mantras describe the priest as a fool if he only parrot-like repeats the mantras not knowing the deep imports thereof. Those who make advancement in knowledge are engaged in seeking and acquiring knowledge; their followers are engaged in spreading knowledge. The others who only repeat the mantras unaware of their deep senses are certainly ignorant fools. The tenth mantra highlights the primacy of logic for analysis and interpretation of the subtle and finer elements of knowledge. In the conferences of the learned, the logical interpreter is honoured by and leads others. Because of his expertise to logically analyse and interprete knowledge he is capable of leading the society along new directions.

Intellect alone facilitates knowledge. The factors that contribute to refinement of intellect are said to be dignitaries (*devatā*) and are welcomed as such. The Sun and the Speech being prime contributors to vision and expression are welcomed as dignitaries. Sages Viśvāmitra and Śyāvāśva praise the dignitary Sun (*Savitṛ*=generator of vision) at 3.62 and 5.82 of the Ṛgveda, respectively, as follows.

"Let us concentrate on the brilliant effulgence of the Sun. He impels our intellect". The Sun shines to light up the world to facilitate vision.

"We sing the glory of the dignified *Savitṛ* to seek his blessings for our intellectual strength".

"Intellectually inspired, the wise honour the dignified *Savitṛ* through sacrifices and mantras".

Similarly implores sage Śyāvāśva, "O! dignified *Savitṛ*, bestow upon us what is for our well-being and dispel all that is inauspicious".

"Inspired and impelled by the dignified *Savitṛ*, let us ponder over whatever is beautiful, to achieve a greater measure of vividity of awareness (*ādhyātmika śakti*)".

Sage Madhuchanda, son of Viśvāmitra, and sage Bharadvāja refer to Sarasvatī (speech) as follows at 1.3.10-12 and 6.61 respectively, in Ṛgveda.

According to Madhuchanda, "The intellect of the fiery (*Pāvakī* is the Vedic name of Sarasvatī) Sarasvatī is complete in all respects. Let her accept the oblations offered by us in sacrifices". (Translator's Note: Let the external object presented to perception be correctly internalized in awareness with appropriate intellectual intervention).

"Let Sarasvatī, who inspires the truthful and awakens the intellect, accept the oblation offered by us in sacrifices".

"Sarasvatī is like the vast ocean. On account of her brilliance she inspires and actuates every one's intellectual acumen".

For Bharadvāja, son of Bṛhaspati, "Sarasvatī is the source of all wealth and of inspiration of every one's intellectual capacity. She protects us by all means".

Says sage Agastya similarly at 1.188 of Ṛgveda, "I address thee all, O' Bhāratī, Ilā and Sarasvati! Inspire us to achieve intellectual excellence, necessary for success everywhere". [Translator's Note: While all the three words (i) Bhāratī, (ii) Ilā and (iii) Sarasvatī generally mean 'speech', their distinctive shades of meanings come from their roots: (i) *Bhṛ*, (ii) *Il* and (iii) *Sṛ* meaning: (i) to acquire, gain, (ii) to keep still, not to move and (iii) to go, move, proceed, respectively. (i) A linguistic expression carves out specific knowledge which is thus acquired, gained. (ii) Knowledge settles down still in mind. It does not move or go away. (iii) It however, goes, moves or proceeds from the speaker to the hearer by means of linguistic expression.]

Whatever is rooted in knowledge comes out of intellect. The Vedas therefore, sing the glory of the facilitators of intellectual acumen that generates knowledge.

We will discuss in the next chapter about the other dignitaries recorded in the Vedas.

Chapter IV

The Vedic Dignitaries (*Devatā,* i.e., the Brilliant/Enlightened Persons)

In the Vedic age, we find, no one has raised any issue as to whether one believes or does not believe in any theory concerning existence or otherwise of God, Creation or Creator, etc. From this angle the Vedas are neither positivist (*āstika*) nor negativist (*nāstika*). They are far from any discussion concerning any variety of theism, mono-theism, polytheism or atheism.

One may ask, who then, are the 'dignitaries (*devatā*)' discussed in the Vedas? Who are the entities addressed while offering oblations and libations in the sacrificial fire? The answer is, many of them are men, our predecessors. Each of them had been a glorious performer. Initiating the aborigine to concepts of order (*ṛta*) and truth (*satya*), the facilitators of human welfare, they reformed him, conferring, as it were, a second birth on him. Having got him established in the societal and ethical culture, they taught him to subscribe thereto with trust (*śraddhā*), steadiness (*niṣṭhā*) and vow (*vrata*). The aborigine had no discrimination, he did not mark out the good from the evil. He fought with his fellow men. He lived like animals in a herd. A refined cultured life in conformity with knowledge, analysis and intellect was unknown to him. The aborigine was far away from societal institutions, social and ethical values, intellectual ability to mark out the good and the evil, generosity, principled life, valour, bravery, forgiveness, sympathy, repentance, felicity, cooperation, education, culture and similar other characteristics appropriate to humanism. Manu taught them the orderliness of these cultural values contributive to human Good. So the aborigine came to be known as 'man' (*mānava*), i.e., the one coming from Manu, but for which he had a beastly life, without education, principles, code of conduct and culture. Initially, the aborigine led a life of nescience, darkness, helplessness, without any code of conduct, analytical discrimination and similar other characteristics. Abiding by only some raw natural instincts, he was roaming around the bushes, scrubs and forests, living in caves or on tree tops, now aggressed, now an aggressor, succumbing to physical and mental ailments and to premature death. The aforesaid dignified glorious predecessors taught men the code of conduct based on moral and logical order that makes a healthy social life possible, if adopted with a firm and determined commitment. The aborigine evolved into the indomitable humanity, consequent upon dispelling the earlier darkness, ushering in intellectual and ethical developments. The Yajurveda declares this in the following verse.

vedāhaṁ etaṁ puruṣaṁ mahāntaṁ
ādityavarṇaṁ tamasaḥ parastāt
taṁ eva viditvā ati mṛtyuṁ eti
na anyaḥ panthā vidyate ayanāya

(Yaju. 31.18 and Śvetāśvatara Up. 3.8)

"I see the all-embracing (*mahāntaṁ*) humanity (*puruṣa*), sparkling with light, as of the Sun, no sooner than the darkness of primitive nescience is dispelled. This aware humanity suffers from no possibility of disintegration (*mṛtyu*). There is no other way to achieve a state, free from disintegration". Every individual has to die and depart. It is the humanity and its limitless progress that has no death. An individual, however, can live beyond his life through his brave, wise progenies. The Veda thus exhorts, *Śṛṇvantu viśve amṛtasya putrāḥ*, "This is thy immortality, behold O! the progeny of the indomitable (humanity)". (Yajurveda and Śvetāśvatara Up. 2.5)

Not only that they initiated the aborigine to truth, education and culture, these dignitaries (*deva*) also worked with a singular devotion to human good and became glorious thereby. They are, therefore, alive for ever in human memory, as beacon-lights of civilization. The *devas* such as Indra, Viṣṇu. Varuṇa, Mitra and others, drove away, destroyed the dark forces such as the *aśuras* or *vṛtras*, i.e., forces counter to the intellectual light of the Vedic culture and sacrifices. [Translator's Note: A *deva* is an enlightening awareness occasioned by linguistic expressions of appropriate literature (*śāstra*). In contrast, *asura* is a blinding instinctive urge occasioned by one's natural biological and psychic disposition to enjoy external objects. *Devāḥ=dīvyateḥ dyotana–arthasya śāstra-udbhāsitā indriya-vṛttayaḥ. Asurāḥ=tat-viparītāḥ, sveṣu eva asuṣu viṣvak-viṣayāsu prāṇana–kriyāsu ramaṇāt svābhāvikyaḥ tama-ātmikā indriya-vṛttaya eva,* Ācārya Śaṅkara's Bhāṣya (SB), Chāndogya Upaniṣad, 1.2.1. *Vṛtra* is supposed to be a personification of darkness; V.S. Apte, Sans.–Eng. Dictionary.

Indra = Idaṁ paśyati iti idandro ... īśvaraḥ. Idandraṁ Indra iti parokṣa-abhidhānena ācakṣate ... saṁvyavahārārthaṁ. Tathā hi parokṣa–nāmagrahaṇapriyā eva hi devaḥ; SB, Aitareya Up. 1.3.14. One, who sees what is referred to by the word 'this' (*idaṁ*), is the seer or the percipient. The percipient is the author (*īśvara*) of the perception. The percipient (*idandra*) is indirectly named (*parokṣa-abhidhāna*) as Indra because an effort to directly describe it must fail. Every description must fall within the sphere of the perception or scene outside the seer. It is in this sense that the dignitaries, i.e., the *deva*s are said to be fond of indirect names for themselves.

Viṣṇu = (*viṣ vyāpane nuk,* V.S. Apte). The word Viṣṇu comes from the root '*viṣ*' meaning 'to pervade'. Every-thing in the world is covered in, is comprehended by and is thus pervaded by knowledge. This feature of knowledge is named Viṣṇu.

Varuṇa = (*Vṛ unan,* V.S. Apte). The word comes from the root *Vṛ* meaning, 'to choose', 'to select'. Knowledge becomes clear and expressive on choosing or selecting the object of knowledge. This feature of knowledge is named *Varuṇa*.

Mitra = (Midyati snihyati, mid tra, mi tra vā, V.S. Apte). The word comes from the roots, '*mid*' or '*mi*'. '*Mid*' means 'to love', 'to feel affection.' The root '*mi*' means 'to measure'. It is often used in the Vedas in the sense of 'to fix in the earth'. One loves to know. Knowledge is clear and specific on being measured, circumscribed or specified. A class-word, can be concretized by 'fixing it on the earth', i.e., by identifying an individual member of the class to which the word applies. This feature of knowledge is named as '*Mitra*', a chosen or selected friend of knowledge. Thus this name usually goes with the name '*Varuṇa*' in the Vedas.

In these senses these words cannot mean any supernatural beings or Gods. These apply to any case of knowing. Their figurative or indirect personifications must, therefore, refer to our thinking forefathers.

Asura – This word has been explained at the commencement of this note.

Vṛtra – The name of a demon killed by Indira. The demon is a personification of darkness or ignorance.]

That is how the dignitaries (*devas*, lights) command our worshipful eulogies. Offering oblations and libations in symbolic sacrificial fire, we address them, so that we get impelled towards their elevating positive characteristics, placing ourselves in their vicinity (*upāsanā*), as it were. That is why the Vedic priests, the *Hota*, the *Udgātā*, the *Brahmā* and the *Ṛtvik*, perform symbolic sacrifices offering oblations in consecrated fire. (Translator's Note: *Hotā*, *Udgātā*, *Brahmā* and *Ṛtvik* are the four principal priests at Vedic sacrifices performing different specific functions.) The flame enlightens, makes things visible and facilitates recollection of names of such things. Fire is the most appropriate choice to symbolize as the 'dispeller of darkness'. It is darkness that is sacrificed to awaken enlightenment. Fire is also an effective disinfectant (*pāvaka*) in addition. There is no knowledge of any visible thing without light. Knowledge contributes to discriminate between what is good and what is evil and consequently to fostering a discriminating faculty. Fire, thus, is the sure source of knowledge, intellect, discrimination and memory. In this view the Sun, the Dawn (*Uṣā*), the Aśvin of two mothers, as well as the Wind (*mātariśvan, mātari antarīkṣe śvayati vardhate,* that which grows in the open, i.e., knowledge grows in an open mind) are facilitators of intellect and dispellers of ailments, and are personified as dignitaries, worthy of our solicitations and eulogies. Aśvin is one and not two. Fire that is born out of friction of two pieces of hard wood is described as of two mothers. Seeing the usefulness of water and breath for sustenance of life, there are also mantras, taking these as dignitaries. The dignitaries have been described in sweet figurative poems suitable for melodious chanting of enchanting audition, as if they were men decorated with ornaments coming to us on horse backs, chariots or otherwise. After the seer sage presents the original ideas finding these useful for human culture, the poets among them got these represented in figurative poetic expressions. Some subsequent purāṇic poets who lacked proper grasp of this poetic literature of the early Vedic poets, says the Rāmāyaṇa, converted the free flow of the crystal-clear-water of the Veda-dharma and culture, to so many dirty, muddy puddles.

'*Sūkta'* means 'well-said'. Melodious eulogies of the utilities of useful things, and of the glorious contributors towards human good, are ever welcome as sources of impelling inspiration. Vedic mantras come in this category. The *Saṁhitās* do not supplicate any supernatural God or God of Gods for his mercy. There is no effort to arouse the compassion of the Creator God towards men crushed and crumbled in dire distress, harassed by the fierce fighting in fetching their livelihood. The *Saṁhitās* are no hoarse cry of distress. They say, 'Let us live a 100 years', 'Let us not lament the departed', 'Let us, instead, work-out ways for a healthy and happy life', 'Let us try, if possible, to extend our lives up to a 120 years', 'Let us not gamble with stakes that may lead to loss of everything'. They also say, 'Since sticking to the same person, till death, as wife or husband, is logically and otherwise beneficial to both, let them live their conjugal life, helping and cooperating with each other till the last breath', 'Let them beget and rear up brilliant progenies'. 'Let no one perish from want of food', the *Saṁhitās* further exhort. These are full of highly reasonable and optimistic views. The Vedas invite one to resolve to establish and to foster these ideals of all-round well-being. 'Dharma' for the Vedas, is a commitment to a universal ethical and societal awareness of propriety and order.

Indra is the ideal warrior. He always ensures the victory of the cultured. He eliminates counterforces, such as the *vṛtras*, *asuras* and *ahis*. (Translator's Note: *Ahi* = A wicked man, a cheat, a rogue. *'Ahi'* is also another name of the aforesaid *vṛtra*.) Applying his weapon, the unbeatable thunderbolt, he smashes the big boulders to clear the path for a free flow of the spring water down from the top of the mountain. He is therefore the first to be invited to the sacrificial site and to be offered the joyful and delighting soma-juice as a libation. Incidentally, we note, this juice is not an intoxicant, a spirituous liquor or *madirā*. Such intoxicants are taken by the *asuras*. During post-Vedic ages it also came to be taken by the warriors. But during the *Saṁhitā* age no spirituous liquor was ever taken by the civilized or cultured (*ārya*) people. The statement 'I salute the departed forefathers who subsist on the soma-juice' (*somapā pitaraṁ vande*), occurring in the Veda refers to the said juice and not to any spirituous liquor. The juice, it is said, flows down from the moon, as if it was the sap of a supposed creeper.

The dignitaries are those individuals that remain alive as ever-inspiring bright luminaries in societal memory. Indra and other dignitaries always give us light, inspiration and all else and they take nothing in return, it is said.

There are also eulogies to Viṣṇu. In three swift steps he drives away the *asuras* and *vṛtras* from all the three worlds, the earth, the atmosphere and beyond, he is eulogized. The word *'Viṣṇu'* literally means 'that which pervades'. He pervades everywhere in no time.

There are also references to dignitaries such as Pūṣan and Aryaman. (Translator's Note: The two words mean the same, the 'Sun', but highlight two different facets of its utility. 'Pūṣan' is that which nourishes, and Aryaman is that which facilitates the submerged to come out of darkness, i.e., light that facilitates optical vision).

All of these dignitaries were of a single head and heart in fostering and nourishing a great civilization and culture and in facilitating an ethical, aesthetic, valuational and logical order of propriety (*ṛta*) that will elevate the culture higher and higher at all times. They are the source of inspiration for humanity. They are the path-makers, the pioneers of progress. They are thus memorable and adorable forever. They thus partake of the same characteristic, working for human good with a single head and heart. They are therefore, together designated as one single dignitary. This is not a theory of theism, of one or of many Gods. Thus says Yajurveda, "He is *agni*, he is *āditya*, he is *vāyu*, he is *candra*, he is *śukra* and he is also *brahmā*. He is the same as the vast expanse of *jala*. He is *prajāpati* as well" (32.1).

[Translator's Note: All these dignitaries are poetic personifications of life–sustaining and enriching elements and of intellectual progress.

Agni (*aṅg* + *ni*, *aṅgati* = *ūrdhvaṁ gacchati*): It is the digestive function that uplifts, converts and promotes the raw food to life-sustaining vital force.

Āditya (*aditeḥ apatyaṁ*): The Sun, a son of *aditi*. There is also a concept of twelve *ādityas* representing

The Sun in the twelve months of a year, the sure source of light in all seasons, the light of intellect.

Vāyu (*Vā* + *yuk*, *Vā* = To blow): The vital air, the breath.

Candra (*Cand* + *rak*, *cand* = To shine, rejoice): The bliss of intellectual awareness.

Śukra (*Śuc* + *rak*, *Śuc* = To brighten, illuminate): The bright, radiant, shining vitality.

Brahmā (*Bṛṁh* + *manin* = Brahman. It takes the form *Brahmā* in masculine. Bṛṁh = To grow, increase): It is the intellect that makes growth of knowledge possible.

Jala (*Jal* = To be rich): It is water that sustains and enriches life.

Prajāpati: The source of procreation, the vital force.]

All these forces work for human good as if with a singular determination. This does not mean that there is only one God. It is a case of many individuals working with a singular devotion, a common destination and a stable steadfastness towards human good. There is a story in Ṛgveda, 10.72.6., that Aditi, the daughter of *Dakṣaprajāpati*, begot all dignitaries and men, and that the dignitaries raised a huge wave of dust while dancing together, holding each other's hands, right after their birth. This indicates that these dignitaries were of a single head and heart. This is neither mono-theism (*ekeśvara-vāda*) nor a theory of one substance (*eka-tattva-vāda*). There is no theory of creation nor any concept of a creator in the Veda. On the earth in the solar family there is gradual evolution, starting with appearance of water everywhere and then rising up of lands from beneath the vast ocean carving out distinct lands and oceans. The aquatic bacteria gradually evolved into aquatic insects and worms, followed by further evolution of grass, scrubs, plants and trees on land. In course of time appeared a rotative regularity of seasons. It was followed by appearance of a variety of animals, birds, beasts and men. Those who departed after doing some good to their families and to their immediate environs, became forefathers (*pitṛ*s) and those who struggled for the good of humanity as a whole became dignitaries (*devatā*), it is said. Both the forefathers and the dignitaries are contributors to human progress. Sacrificial rites are meant to derive inspiration from the examples of the dignitaries. To start with, one has to offer his animal instinct as an oblation in the sacrificial function and has to take a second birth (*dvijatva*) of humanity, free from the beastly instincts. This is a concept of societal evolution clearly indicated in the Vedas. The Vedic approach is thus intellectual and scientific. There is no fanatic religious dogmatism. There is no creator of the world. There is no mysterious theory of creation of things from nothing. There are no stories of ghosts and chimeras as may be found in later religious traditions. There is no story of a benevolent God or of a mysterious theory of creation as one may come across in later *purāṇa*s. We will build upon these ideas in some more detail in the following Chapters on 'The

Verse to the Person' and 'The Song to the Soil' (Ch.V and IX).

The Vedas address the dignitaries as co-travellers and companions. The Ṛgveda claims of Indra, not to part company. "Thou art the initiator and preserver of the order of propriety (*ṛta*). We are devoutly observing the order and truth. You owe your dignity and brilliance to your leading the wars and to ensuring our victory at all times. You cannot now depart from that path leaving us alone. Go on helping us. So we will ever eulogise you, so your dignity and glory will continue to shine. You have no other way to retain your greatness. Do not part our company. Go on securing our victory in all our struggles."

Man evolved into a second birth of a socio-ethical being having been steadily established in logical and ethical order of propriety (*ṛta*) and truth, observing austere meditation. One who abides by certain principles can distinguish between what is good and what is evil so that he adopts the former and avoids the latter. It is only then that one resolves to pursue the good, to repent a mistake and an instinctive unfair conduct. Principles prevent instinctive capriciousness and its consequent conflicts. One becomes conscientious and free from instinctive urge. One gets steady in discharging one's duties and responsibilities. One commands self-control in one's principled conduct, one earns a principled personality. That is why Indra is welcome as the path-finder of human freedom on account of his singular contribution of the concept of the logical and ethical order of propriety. He is also eulogized as the 'bestower of awareness' (*ātmadā*) and the 'bestower of worth' (*baladā*) because he has bestowed on us our capacity of self-control. Thus the awareness (*ātman*) referred to in the Vedas is distinct from the 'substantive disembodied spirit' (*ātman*=soul) referred to in the *purāṇas*, as well as in the later religious literatures. This later 'spirit' is immortal. Casting away the current body it adopts new ones in conformity with its dispositions (*saṁskāra*) and desires (*vāsanā*). It may also go to the Heaven or to the Hell as ordained by God, on account of its good or evil deeds. Since it is immortal, it has to undergo rebirth on conclusion of its sojourn in the Heaven or in the Hell. But the Vedic 'awareness' is a gift from Indra. It was blunt in the primitive. It neither roams around after the end of the body nor adopts a new body. But 'humanity', when it is steadily established on the principles of propriety, order and truth, becomes intemporal and enduring. Humanity can only progressively evolve. This possibility of progress is intemporal and limitless. Annihilation of 'humanity' is impossible unless it departs from propriety, order and truth. [Translator's Note: Śaṅkara derives the word *'ātman'* from the following three roots, covering the whole range of knowledge. The word may mean a logical entity, timelessness, simplicity, consciousness and openness being its basic nature (*nitya-śuddha-buddha-mukta-svabhāvo*). For brevity, however, we translate it as 'awareness'. "*āpnoteḥ atteḥ atateḥ vā*", SB. Ai. Up. 1.1.1.

āp = To obtain, attain, get; *ad* = To eat, devour, digest; *at* = To go, walk, obtain, bind. Thus *ātman* is the rudimentary 'simple-awareness' that takes upon itself a predication, on (a) reaching out (*āp*) to the reference, (b) subsuming it to a generalization (*ad*) and (c) predicating a class-word (*at*) thereto].

The dignitaries are individuals who gained their dignity on account of their contribution to the common good of humanity. They live forever through our eulogical praises to their glory. Ṛgveda (10.72) highlights the point. "We will describe in detail how the dignitaries came into being, so that our progenies will see them in the same light as we have seen". "The seers (*Brahmaṇaḥ pati* = the authors of the Vedas) have forged, hammered them out, complete in all respects, even as a smith works out his smithery. The dignitaries were non-beings before they came into being". No dignitary was recognized as such, to start with. The authors of the Vedas presented them as dignitaries by eulogizing them as directors of human destiny. "Progress in all directions commenced only after these dignitaries thus came into being. Then followed the intellectual activity of defining the world and of its quarters. *Aditi* came out of *Dakṣa* and *Dakṣa* came out of *Aditi*". (Translator's Note: *Dakṣa* = Able, competent, expert, clever, skillful. *Aditi* = Free, not tied, boundless, unlimited, inexhaustible, entire, unbroken, happy, pious, mostly Vedic in all these senses, represented both as mother and daughter of *Dakṣa*.) "Yes, *Aditi* did come into being. She is your (*Dakṣa's*) daughter. Then came out from her the intemporal dignitaries, all of them actuated with a single objective."

The idea here is that after the primitive homo sapiens found themselves as members of a single human race the pioneering path-finders among them got recognized as dignitaries. The idea that *Dakṣa* and *Aditi* were the sources of each other indicates that it is reasonable to assume a gradual evolution of the progressive development of the human race. 'Who were the parents of all?', is not a valid question. It is in order to bring out the invalidity of such a question that the Veda declares that *Dakṣa* and *Aditi* are the sources of each other. The dignitaries are the friends, philosophers and guides, the well-wishers of the human race. They do good to the humanity at large, at all times. The Vedas indicate their duties to them, even as one alerts one's friend to keep awake or to help one in a certain definite regard. In this vein, Ṛgveda alerts Indra, "O' Indra! be ever on the watch beside us, to help us out at the time of our need. Love us as a companion. Keep beside us during the time of our dark despair till the bright light dawns, (6.24). Be well-disposed towards us, O' Mitra! O' Varuṇa! O' Aryaman! O' Indra! O' Bṛhaspati! O' all-permeating Viṣṇu! All of you remain well-disposed towards us at all times, (1.90)".

Indra is the ideal warrior always promoting the refined (*ārya*) culture and society. He has limitless excellence and courage in eliminating counter-forces. The Ṛgveda is therefore replete with frequent eulogies to him. His characteristics eulogized in these verses enable us to make out a clear conception of all these dignitaries. For this purpose, we repeat below some of the names with which he is addressed.

Indra, Ojiṣṭha (of the highest strength), Śuṣmitaṁ (of the best prowess), Inatama (most virulent), Saviṣṭha (all-powerful), Nṛtama (best man), Rathitama (best warrior on a chariot), Mahiṁṣṭha (of the greatest kindness), Abhṛkatama (best sympathizer), Satāṁ jyeṣṭhatama (the best of good men), Variṣṭha (most gentle), Vipratama (the best of wisemen), Śivatama (most auspicious), Preṣṭha (dearest), Pitṛtama pitṛṇāṁ (the most loving patriarch), Antama (nearest), Nandintama (most pleasant), Eka, Kevala, Para, Parama, Prathama, Pāvaka, Pātā, Trāṇa, Mahān, Sunīti, Śūra, Vṛtrahā, Jetā-aparājitaḥ (the winner ever undefeated), Pati, Gaṇapati (the leader of the masses), Cāru (handsome), Citratama, Śriyaṁ-vasānā (embellished), Vapu (of beauty personified), Sakhā, Damunā (friend of the householder), Veṇaḥ (of pleasing disposition), Maghavā (one who gives gracious gifts), Kavi, Nṛtu (a dancer in action), Savaṣā-dakṣiṇāvān (beauty of prowess). It is also said that Indra finds expression everywhere in diverse ways in a variety of forms and features. He appears in all forms, it is said.

We therefore conclude that the dignitaries are those who are of the greatest glory among ordinary humans. They are companions and friends of men. They love humanity even as one's parents do.

Chapter V

The Verse to the Person (*Puruṣa Sūkta*, Ṛk.10.90.1-16)

The concepts of 'The Person (*Puruṣa*)', 'The Intellectual splendour (*Virāj*)', and 'The Womb of All Possibilities (*Hiraṇyagarbhaḥ* = gold-mine)'

As already indicated (Ch.I, para.6 and Ch.IV, para. 1), Vedas had no occasion to discuss about creation or the creator. It is rather often clearly indicated that such a discussion is pointless. Keeping this in mind and with a view to re-emphasizing the Veda-dharma, Śaṅkarācārya (Ś) says in his commentary on the Brahma-sūtras, 'A discussion about creation is pointless (*sṛṣṭi-cintakāḥ nirarthakāḥ*)'. A discussion about creation is like trying to reach a mirage. That something (*sattā*) is the case, is a necessary assumption that precedes any search for truth. No question concerning truth or otherwise of anything can arise without this assumption. [Translator's Note: While this particular statement, '*Sṛṣṭi* ...', could not be traced, statements such as ('*Kuta eva sṛṣṭi*?', B.S.S.B. 2.1.22) 'How does arise a question concerning creation?', and many others in all of Ś's commentaries corroborate the point.] The Vedic seer conceives that the earth, the atmosphere, the outer space, the Sun, the Moon, the stars and the planets all precede the birth of the dignitaries and men. Everything on earth was subject to a universal order. This order is named '*ṛta*'. This order regulates the timely occurrence of the spring with the breeze from the south, with its seasonal events, harvesting of grains, flowering of vines and fruiting of trees. In the same order the clouds form with the vapours from the seas and the rains fall to replenish the rivers and the lakes. The rains promote growth of vegetation to sustain life of men and of the human world.

"Order indeed is honey,
It secretes from the breeze,
It secretes from the rivers ..."
*"Madhu vātā ṛtāyate
Madhu kṣaranti sindhavaḥ ..."* etc.

Life springs up on the earth facilitated by regular replenishment of the rains, the breeze, the vegetations and other wherewithal. Men and dignitaries grow up on such an earth. Humanity, i.e., *Puruṣa*, emerges on this fertile platform, the earth. This humanity is initially indiscrete and invisible. It gradually becomes visible and discrete, being categorized into four societal components on the basis of occupational criteria, (i) intellectuals (brāhmaṇa) cultivating their minds, (ii) physically strong warriors (kṣatriya) defending the borders and the culture, (iii) traders (vaiśya) creating wealth through domestic and foreign trade and (iv) manual workers (śūdra). An individual enters into an ethical and societal order after sacrificing its natural beastly life. In this order, humanity gains gradual expression into different categories according to certain professional criteria, after sacrificing its natural indiscreteness. This is the point that 'The Verse to the Person' intends to express in the following manner.

1. "The Person (*Puruṣa* = humanity as a societal entity) has many heads, eyes and feet (i.e., many organs of sense and action). It pervades the whole range of knowledge. It has the possibility to grow beyond its contours at all times, i.e., this possibility is always wider by ten finger-breadths (a finger-breadth=eight barley corns)". Gaining an awareness of cognitive, conative and affective sense of propriety (*ṛta*) through an orderly societal living, humanity comes to have more and more knowledge. As said earlier, since language and knowledge was possible only through collaborative interaction of many societal participants, the store-house of knowledge becomes richer and richer, through the same process. Successive generations learn the existing knowledge to extend it further. Fields of learning proliferate leading to growth of appropriate institutions for teaching and research. By the force of the collaborative efforts of its members, humanity overwhelms the rest of the biological world.
2. "Evolving out of their primitive causal condition, individual members of this class of men are concrete instances of humanity, consuming fruits, roots and meets etc. The concept 'Person', however, covers humanity, past, present and

future, and is thus, obviously, unbreakable (*amṛta*)".

3. "Membership of the class of men is the worth (*mahimā*) of an individual. The concept 'humanity' is wider in connotation. Only a small fraction (literally a fourth) of its possible members constitutes the world and the greater part (literally three-fourths) remains as illuminating (*dyotanātmaka*) possibilities." All the past, present and future members will aggregate to only a small part of its infinite possible members. [TN: This Ṛk mantra is quoted by the Śāmavedic Chāndogya Upaniṣad at 3.12.6. Expanding, Ś. says, "*Vikāra-lakṣaṇāt ... vācāraṁbhaṇa-mātrāt ... mahattara parama-artha-satya-rūpo avikāraḥ puruṣaḥ ... sarva- pūraṇāt, puri-śayanāt ca ... tripāt-amṛtaṁ puruṣākhyaṁ samastasya ... ātmano divi, dyotanavati, svātmani avasthitaṁ*". "While the 'discrete (*vikāra*) meaning' of a class-word is exemplified by a member of the class, its 'meaning before such exemplification (*avikāra*)' covers all its possible members. While the former is its cash-value, worked out by linguistic usage (*vācā-āraṁbhaṇaṁ*), the latter is unbreakable (*amṛtaṁ*), and is a simple logical base of a flash (*dyotanavati*) of awareness (*svātmani*) of the user of the class-word. While the former (member) occurs in time and in space, the latter (*puruṣa*) completes (*sarva-pūraṇāt*), its (membership's) valid usage by invisibly residing (*puri śayanāt*), as

it were, within the ambit of the former". As linguistic usage is a human societal function, our author holds that the communicability of a sentence owes ultimately to the axiomatic occurrence of the infinite human society.]

4. "The said greater part (three-fourths) of humanity remains out of the world, free from merits and demerits (i.e., the future is not yet realized). The small part (one-fourth) constitutes the world for all generations. Those who constitute the world also fall into two categories, those in the present concrete world (*sāśana* = eating) and those in the past historical world (*anaśana* = not eating)". The former covers men in concrete factual interaction (*sāśana*) and the latter covers the departed ones including the dignitaries etc., without such concrete factual interaction (*anaśana*).

5. "Humanity evolves its intellectual splendour (*virāj*) that gives rise to the clearer concept of humanity as a Person (*puruṣa*). This 'Person' supersedes, sublates its primitive brutality and habitat." The primitive brutal man takes a second birth into a value-based societal humanity occupying the whole of its primitive world and building it up into a suitable human settlement (*pura*) of a civilized society. The Saṁskṛt word '*Puruṣa*' means the one that lives in a settlement (*puri śete*). The uncivilized brute becomes a member of a civilized human society when it lays the foundation of societal upliftment due to its

organized living in a civilized society. As we will see in the next Chapter, this 'Person', i.e., 'humanity', measures up to six finger-breadths, i.e., humanity is said to consist of five non-Vedic cultures in addition to the Vedic (*ārya*) one.

6. "The dignitaries initiated the human society into sacrificial functions. Spring was the libation, summer the fuel and autumn, the oblation in such sacrifices." In the spring, summer and autumn seasons are produced enough milk and ghee, fuel-wood and fruits etc., respectively, as symbolic sacrificial offerings for the sustenance of humanity.

7. "The primitive brute is burnt in the intellectual sacrificial fire and is sacrificed by the dignitaries (*devāḥ*) and by the matured persons (*siddha*) and the seers (*ṛṣi*), and in the process, is consecrated into the human culture." The beastly man is initiated into a life of propriety, order (*ṛta*) and truth (*satya*) and is got organized into certain professional types. As these are psychological and attitudinal developments brought about by appropriate instructions (*śikṣā*), cultivation (*saṁskāra*) and dedication (*dīkṣā*), the sacrifice is always intellectual (*mānasa yajña*). To sacrifice is to genuinely part with. The Veda indicates that primitive brutality is sacrificed as an oblation to the sacred intellectual sacrificial fire and humanity gets organized into the four broad aptitudinal professional types. The primitive,

uncultured, violent brutality is sacrificed. One adopts a determined dedicated approach to an orderly societal, value-based and truthful living for humanity to prevail.

8. "It is only after this comprehensive (*sarvahut*) sacrifice that the societal man (*Puruṣa*) works out dairy products as well as the creatures living around human habitats, in forests and in the atmosphere." Men gradually learn to domesticate certain animals as cattles etc. They also evolve appropriate skills to sort out and lebel them as well as certain others found elsewhere. (Translator's Note: Pragmatic objective awareness evolves after eradication of primitive prejudices).
9. "Similarly after the said comprehensive sacrifice, did evolve the Ṛk, the Śāma, the metres and the Yajuḥ" (Translator's Note: Knowledge as a logical entity can emerge only after one frees oneself from the stranglehold of natural psycho-biological primitive prejudices and pre-dispositions.)
10. "Consequent upon similar sacrifice, do evolve the horses, the other animals with teeth on both sides, the cows, the goats and the rams". Men sacrifice their limited perception to domesticate these animals for a greater societal use. They also gradually expand their knowledge and learn newer and newer skills to process and preserve various dairy products for subsequent use.

11. "Humanity (*Puruṣa*) gradually comes to be seen as formed by various segments. What are these? Who is its speech organ? Who are its arms, thighs and feet?" These questions do not seek to dissect a physical body into so many limbs or organs. It is a case of mental (*mānasika*) categorization of men according to their professional activities occasioned by societal interactions. The word 'Person (*Puruṣa*)' has been seen as 'The Glorious Creator of the World' by all the commentators, from Yāska (5th century B.C.) to Sāyaṇa (14th century, A.D.). But this and the next mantras are clearly intelligible only if the word is taken as the 'societal humanity', because it is then alone that a question concerning a segmentation (*katidhā*) is sensible. It is also found that in 'The Verse to the Śūdra and to Agronomy' (Ch.VI), and in 'The Ode to Harvesting' (*ibid.*), the group of toiling hands is termed as 'The Field-person (*Kṣetrapuruṣa*)' who is exhorted to exert its hundred hands and thousand feet in agriculture and harvest. The word 'Person' thus expresses a definite meaning, 'a group of men/ women'. We therefore take the word in that sense here.
12. "Brāhmaṇa, Kṣatriya, Vaiśya and Śūdra, respectively, are its speech-organ, arms, thighs and feet." [Translator's Note: The learning of the brāhmaṇa, the vigour of the warrior (kṣatriya), the wealth-creating skill of the merchant (vaiśya) and the manual effectiveness of the śūdra are,

respectively, the speech-organ, the arms, the thighs and the feet of humanity seen as a person].

13. "The Moon is its psyche, the Sun its sight, air its breath and fire and Indra are its speech." These are indicative of knowledge, life and society. One perceives (psyche=moon) things in light (knowledge=sun=eye). Air is breathed in and out. Speech exudes fire of intellectual brilliance and also expresses rules and regulations (Indra).

14. "Its navel is the atmosphere (*antarīkṣa*), head the sky (*dyuloka*), feet the earth (*bhūmi*) and ears are the directions (*diśaḥ*)". One stands up on the earth. The active and intelligent humanity (Person) sorts out and labels this support for its feet as the earth, the space above the head as the sky and the area above the navel as the atmosphere etc.

15. "The dignitaries go on expanding the scope of the intellectual sacrifice of seven circumferences (*paridhi*) and 21 fire-woods (*samidha*) to tame the beastly primitive person." [Translator's Note: The scope of the intellectual sacrifice is ever expanding. The seven concentric circles symbolize the ever-expanding scope that engulfs all possible limitations, cognitive, conative and affective, thrice the seven circles, symbolized by twenty-one fire-woods burnt away. To bring home the point, Chāndogya Upaniṣad (V.18.1) cautions against taking 'awareness', as if it were a psychological entity entirely defined by this or that sensation

(*paricchinna-ātma-buddhiḥ*, Ś), even as a born-blind, unaware of the meaning of the class-word 'elephant', tends to define it entirely in terms of his limited non-visual perceptions (*hasti-darśana iva jātyandhāḥ*, Ś).]

16. "The sacrifice is also sacrificed by the dignitaries. That is the very first principle of intellectual progress. The land of enlightened brilliance of the dignitaries and of the matured achievers of the past also, thus, becomes the abode of those who work to cultivate humanity." Primitive natural brutality is sacrificed as a libation to build up the concept of cultured humanity, consisting of complementary professional classes. 'Libation' and 'sacrifice' are not two separate concepts here.

'The Verse to the Person' of the Yajurveda also similarly adds, "I came to know the all-embracing 'humanity' of solar-like brightness highlighted by knowledge no sooner than the darkness of primitive ignorance is dispelled. This aware humanity suffers from no possibility of disintegration. There is no way to a factual state free from disintegration of the body." Humanity is deathless. Its intellectual progress is eternal. An individual is a progeny of this all-encompassing humanity. The former partakes of the immortality of the latter. The pioneers and path-makers of humankind are thus immortal. An individual as such has to die and to go to the World of the Manes (*pitṛloka*).

'The Verse to the Person' presents no theory of creation. It holds that the individuals who initiate the primitive brute unto the orderly life based on truth and self-control are the builders of 'humanity'. These path-makers of order and truth live forever as bright luminaries in the societal memory, the World of Light (*devaloka*). It is the primitive that forges ahead from progress to progress having mastered the art of acquiring knowledge through use of language and through skillful activities, consequent upon intellectual progress beyond their predecessors. Such being the nature of 'humanity' it is impossible that there can be any retrogression, instead of progress, at any stage. Humanity has taken a second birth, imbibing sociability, value-based life and culture, after sacrificing its narrow brutal primitivity. Yama teaches him to remain prepared to happily invite death after completing a long and fruitful life. Death at a matured age opens up the opportunity for one's successors to usher in a greater progress. Death thus is a stair step, up for progress. Yama becomes a dignitary by happily embracing death. One who sacrifices himself for societal well-being and leads humanity along the path of the light of knowledge lives forever in societal memory. This World of Light (*devaloka*) and the World of the Manes (*pitṛloka*), the two worlds have thus been conceived to accommodate the men of the past.

The primitive man-beast lives in caves, is violent and eats even human flesh. He is without education and without culture. Those who introduce him to the culture of propriety, order and truth, are ever honourable. Knowledge expands only in an educated and civilized society. On sacrifice of primitivity and on adoption of a cultured life, one graduates into a second birth of an integrated societal life (*amṛtatva*).

While reiterating the validity of this thesis of the Veda-dharma, Ś indicates that use of language, *śabda* or *śastra*, is the source of all knowledge (*śaṁsanāt kathanāt śāstraṁ*, Gītā Bhāṣya). (Translator's Note: We have yet to come across this particular expression. The following expressions, however, corroborate the point.

i) *Śrutvā* = *dṛṣṭvā* = *uktvā*, II-29. Heard = seen = told.
ii) *Jñānaṁ* = *śāstroktapadārthānāṁ parijñānaṁ*, VI-8. To know = to have a clear perception of the meanings of the words used.
iii) *Śāstraṁ* = *mayā uktaṁ*, XVIII-67. *Śāstra* = what I have said.

According to V.S. Apte, the word *'śāstra'* comes from the root *'śās'*, meaning, 'To tell, communicate, inform'.) There is no knowledge without use of language. Language communicates and thereby refines and expands knowledge. Knowledge is imperishable, does not disintegrate (*amṛta*). On achieving knowledge, humanity crosses over the physical world of perishable commodities. There is no creator of the world, says Ś. He says in his gloss on the Brahmasūtras, 'A discussion about creation is pointless, *Sṛṣṭicintakāḥ nirarthakāh*. (Translator's Note: See translator's note in the first paragraph of this chapter). Denial of existence, e.g., by some Buddhists, is unintelligible. Existence (*sattā*) cannot extinguish. The knower gives expression to the unexpressed existence, by means of sortal and or characterizing linguistic labels (*nāmarūpa*). Existence cannot be otherwise comprehended. It is without any description and therefore is without any comprehension before such labelling. That the Vedas are thus entirely about knowledge, gets reiterated through Advaita-vedānta of Ś. He expounds the truths of 'The Verse of Knowledge (Ṛk.10.71.1 to 11 at Ch.III, Features of Knowledge)' and of 'The Verse to the Person' of the Ṛgveda through this simple logic of his Advaita-vedānta.

The four societal segments hinted above are based entirely on aptitudinal and professional (*guṇa, karma*) categorization. Emergence of a professional categorization of the members of the society is also equally unavoidable. Someone concerns himself with knowledge, research and teaching, engaging himself in mental activities to sharpen his intellect. His profession is mental and intellectual. Society needs his services because he not only educates the uneducated but also opens up new vistas of knowledge. Language is the function of speech and is the foundation of rationalism. Therefore, speech (*mukha*) is the knower, brāhmaṇa, who thus represents the speech organ of the society. He is brāhmaṇa because he knows the in-depth meaning of Brahma, i.e., the Veda. He is not a brāhmaṇa by virtue of his birth in a certain family. He is so by his profession and occupation. Similarly, a warrior, kṣatriya, is one who learns the art to protect the nation, the humanity and the culture, dharma. War was fought manually or by simple handheld weapons calling for enough physical strength of the arms. The warrior, i.e., the kṣatriya is thus said to represent the arms of the society. The professional merchant, the vaiśya, contributes to the growth of overall wealth of the society through internal and external trade and through movement of goods from surplus areas to deficit areas. These three types of professional functions need services from manual labour against wages. The śūdra is one whose profession it is to provide manual service to the society. The categorization of the members of the society into the said four types is thus based entirely on their perceived aptitudes and occupations and is not at all attributable to their birth in any family. To corroborate the point, we have the verse number 9.112 of the Ṛgveda stating that different members of the same family may adopt different professions. The author of the verse, Śiśu of the Angirasa family states, "I am a poet. My father is a physician. My mother husks grains for sale. Like a milkman caring for all his cattle, we care for our different professions to meet the needs of the family". Śiśu as a poet is a seer, a brāhmaṇa. His father can also be a brāhmaṇa on account of his medical profession. His mother is a merchant, vaiśya, for, she processes grains by husking, making these suitable for sale for a profit. From this Vedic instance of various members of the same family adopting different professional occupations we conclude that the said classification is based on the perceived criterion of one's aptitude and profession, and not on one's birth to a certain family.

None of the said four classes are higher or lower in societal esteem. Speech, arms, thighs and feet symbolize different functions of the societal organism. These are not upper or lower limbs of an individual. The idea here is that of a suitable classification of a member of the society according to his perceived profession. A manual worker symbolizes the feet of the society on account of his profession to support the society through manual work, while earning his livelihood. Yajurveda states at *Adhyāya* 26, "I will explain these invaluable Vedic ideas to the public, to brāhmaṇas, to the warriors (*rājanya*), śūdras and vaiśyas, all alike, as well as to the locals and to the aliens". This shows that these segments were of equal status. It may also be noted that the verse states the names 'śūdra' and 'vaiśya' at the third and the fourth places. The occupational segmentation is not a hierarchical stratification of the society. The accidental mention of one name after another is not meant to convey any weightage of societal status.

That the manual worker renders a valuable service is clearly demonstrated in 'The Verse to the Śūdra and to Agronomy', Ch.VI. People working in a group in the field, i.e., the śūdra as a group is addressed as the 'Field Person (*Kṣetrapuruṣa*)'. As the śūdra is free from sacrificial rituals (*ajajvan*) the land owners go to his residence to invite him for field-work. These workers come in groups, with hundreds and thousands of hands, to work together as a single 'Field-person', making labour-intensive agriculture and harvest possible. We will discuss this in more detail, citing Vedic verses in the next chapter. Brāhmaṇas, kṣatriyas and vaiśyas were, thus, to approach the śūdra at his residence offering him appropriate wages. The śūdra is sought after by the rest of the society, according him full societal status. But for his occupation, no one is śūdra by birth. He is neither untouchable nor low in hierarchy. The name 'śūdra' precedes the name 'vaiśya' in many Vedic verses. This does not mean that the vaiśya is lower in rank. All the members of the society, of the four occupational types, are its equally useful components. Unaccustomed to the specific education and culture involved in abstract intellectual subtleties concerning sacrifices, the śūdra cannot participate in such endeavours. As a result, he has adopted the occupation of earning his livelihood from wages against his manual work. The intellectuals, the warriors and the merchants are called 'twice-born (*dvija*)' due to their graduation from appropriate education and culture. By the age of 8 to 12 years of the child, an intellectual performs his child's investiture (*vrata*). The warriors and the merchants do so by 10 to 16 and 14 to 24 years, respectively, for their children. On investiture, they are required to live with the teacher at his residence until they thoroughly learn and imbibe the Vedic education and culture. A child of these groups, who grows up without such investiture and education, has no occasion to learn the Vedic education and is called uninvested, (*vrātya = vrātāt, samūhāt cyavati*), not accustomed to Vedic education. An uninvested person without any education and training can be harmful to himself as well as to societal well-being. By the mere force of his family tradition, he may engage in intellectual, military or commercial activities, without any scruples. He is lower than śūdra in societal rank. While one can accept manual services from the śūdra, it is inauspicious even to look at the face of an uninvested. One may rather suffer acute grief and calamity than accept any assistance from an uninvested. But a warrior or a merchant could marry a daughter of a manual worker. Manual workers were also leading conjugal life, whereas no one will give away his daughter to an uninvested. The manual worker is not lower in status in any manner. As everyone needs manual services, everyone is grateful to the manual worker. Particularly in agriculture, the manual worker is entitled to nine parts out of sixteen of the produce, towards his wages. We will come back to these ideas in the next chapter. Although a śūdra could not intellectually participate in sacrificial technicalities, he was entitled to be present nearby. The sacrifices those days were simple, charming and congenial. In this context, the meaning of the word 'yajña' is 'To liaise'. It fosters a close liaison among all the four professional segments. The śūdra was unaware of how to pronounce and sing the Veda-mantras, how to offer the oblations and how to function as an overseer. His services were solicited to collect various materials, being present at the site. Even though he is called 'a non-participant in sacrificial technicalities (*ayajvan*)', the śūdra is not untouchable in any sense. As an essential component of the society, he is of equal status as others, and on occasions, particularly in agriculture, the śūdra is accorded a higher status.

Chapter VI

Professional Segmentation of the Society

We said earlier (Ch.II and III) that use of language alone is the appropriate method that enables one, to clearly formulate a quest for truth, to expand knowledge and to preserve it for posterity. Knowledge becomes clear and expressive through language, so that others can understand, debate, interpret, rectify and refine. Language facilitates and is facilitated by many people living together and communicating with each other. I use a word, say, 'tree' to mean a certain type of object. If others also do the same the word gains currency, a linguistic usage comes into being and language gets enriched. No language is entirely private. Private knowledge is no knowledge. All by myself, I cannot bring any linguistic usage into currency. Linguistic usage is impossible, is frustrated, if others do not follow what I say, and I do not follow what others say. I see a thing and call it a 'tree' today. Next day I may call it by another name. Suppose I try to recollect the word I used yesterday, and accidentally I feel, I succeed in recollecting it. There is no way to ascertain if what I so recollect is free from error or it is otherwise. I point at a thing which others call a 'tree'. I call it by any other name, someone will correct me. This is how linguistic usage firms up. Over a period of time, usage can also absorb many shades of meanings and can branch out to convey new meanings in different contexts, for the sake of elegant and effective communication. Knowledge, therefore, is the gift to us from the light (*devī*) of speech (*vāk*). Speech is like a fenceless fertile floral field where fresh flowers of knowledge blossom forth day in and day out. One who engages himself in analysis of, and investigation into, epistemological issues is said to be sitting close to the light of speech (*vākdevī upāsaka*). In this view of the matter, linguistic usage can take place only in a societal environment where many people communicate with each other. Consequently, the need to express one's ideas through language also forms the foundation upon which a societal life is built up. 'Human society' is designated as 'The Person Infinite (*Mahān Puruṣa*)' or 'The Supreme Person (*Parama Puruṣa*)' because it is based on intellectual evolution and is capable of using, evolving and pioneering linguistic expressions. It is the societal life alone where concepts such as language, knowledge, ethics, discrimination, personality and so on, are meaningful. It is the human society alone that is by nature open at all times to more and more progress and has consequently achieved higher and higher development. The population of other living beings can shrink or can become extinct. But there is, and is bound to be a gradual growth and enrichment of humanity which is deathless and is unextinguishable. The children of the succeeding generations inherit opportunities of greater chances of health, strength, education and intellect, than the preceding generations. They are thus the inheritors of integration (*amṛtasya putrāḥ*) having been born to a society which is by nature progressive at all times. Education thus becomes an essential ingredient of societal institution. The more the storehouse of knowledge expands, the more the contents and methods of education proliferate without limit. Education takes place through learning and teaching. Educated seniors encourage their wards to acquire more and more learning under the discipline and guidance of the teachers over an appropriate period of time. This system of learning and teaching was one of the most valuable institutions during the Vedic age. On initiation (*upanayana* = admission into the curriculum) a student is entrusted to the teacher for a course of study spreading over a period as long as twelve years. During this period the student lives with the teacher in his residential school, *gurukula*, the teacher's precincts. On conclusion of the course, the graduate attends the convocation where matured parting advices are imparted. He is then allowed to return home for the life of a householder. The teacher is himself a householder. Married, he lives with his family in his *gurukula*, which is thus very congenial for the resident students, boys and girls, who live a life of discipline under the close supervision of the teacher and his wife. The precinct is thus an eminently suitable place, for living a life of a learner (*brahmacaryāśrama*) of practical behavioral discipline. Deep concentration, strict discipline and wide application are essential components of this method of education. Assiduous application of the implications of whatever is learnt leads to a sharpening of intellectual and retaining capacity. Fire lights and enlightens and is thus the symbol of enlightenment. To focus this constantly in mind it was customary for the teacher to commence every session with offering oblations to the sacrificial fire. The student is called upon to fetch fire-wood (*samidha*). He also takes the cows for grazing, so there will be enough ghee for libations (*āhuti*) and enough milk to be offered (*naivedya*) to the fire and later to be consumed by the inmates. The student also goes round to collect alms enough to maintain the institution. The flame of the sacrificial fire facilitates academic sessions in the evenings and in the dawns, where all the participants congregate. This fire is therefore the coordinator (*yajña*) of these sessions contributing to a rapt rapport among the teacher and the students. It was an essential duty of the school to tame and channelize the students' natural primordial instinctive urge of the flesh to a greater and more durable and enduring trait of intellectual commitment forming the foundation of an orderly life of the householder of the future. The student's physical body becomes strong stout and rugged due to continuous exercise involved in roaming round the forests in search of dry fire-wood, carrying it back in head-loads and sitting close to the fire with close attention and participation in academic sessions. Cow-ghee when burnt in fire generates enough oxygen. Long academic sessions around this powerful source of oxygen facilitates a balanced physical and mental health. Living a life of strict discipline, of long exposure near the sacrificial fire, of use of bark as his vest, a life of alround hardship, the student is prepared to face any hard work in future, even as gold glitters better after it is burnt. The school trains the student to remain ever prepared to lay down his life, if needed, in the war-field, fighting to safe-guard the dharma and the culture. He is thus called 'poison-eater (*viṣabhuk*)', as if he has shared and digested poison with Yama, the dignitary of death. He is also called 'fire resistant (*tapasvī*)' because of his prolonged hard life in the residential school. The words 'burning fire (*tapa*)', 'vow (*vrata*)' etc., mean that one intently engages oneself in deep concentration etc., while living a hard life of austerity and self-control. He is therefore named as 'a self-controller (*brahmacārī*)', 'a poison eater (*viṣabhuk*)', 'a world citizen (*viśvakṛt*)' and a 'vow observer (*vratacārī*)'. 'World-citizen' implies that one is capable of building up a new humanity due to one's effective skill to introduce new ethical values of propriety and order (*ṛta*) to the old society of darkness. 'World' here does not mean a physical entity. The famous Vedic statement, 'Listen O! the children of the imperishable world (*śṛṇvantu viśve amṛtasya putrāḥ*)' uses the word 'world' in this sense of 'all members of humanity'. Engaged in intellectual evolution, in quest of knowledge and in imparting knowledge, these students grow up to form an essential limb of the Vedic society. One who is engaged in epistemological research and in extension of knowledge, is designated as 'brāhmaṇa'. He is conversant with the Vedic fundamentals. Since

Veda is Brahma, the knower of Veda is '*Brahmā*' or 'Brāhmaṇa'. This *Brahmā* is not a Master Creator (*Īśvara*) of the physical world. He knows the defined glossarial (*nirukta*) meanings of Vedic expressions, resulting from deep concentration of mind. No one is a brāhmaṇa by birth. One could be so only on account of one's profession of deep intellectual preoccupation. As it is the nature of intellect that anything to be intelligible has to be verbalized in speech, the brāhmaṇa represents the speech organ of humanity as if it was a person (*puruṣa*). No one takes 'brāhmaṇa' as a higher caste on account of a wrong analogy that the brāhmaṇa was born from the speech organ located on the upper part of the body. The physical location of the speech organ is beside the point. The idea is that speech and the speech organ are closely linked. Therefore, one whose occupation is to remain engaged in research into Vedic and common linguistic usages and the consequent intellectual awareness, is seen as representing the speech organ (*mukha*) of the societal humanity.

While intellectual and ethical values are essential for societal evolution, equally essential is the value of physical force of the warrior and of the king, the leading warrior (kṣatriya), to maintain internal order, to punish the unsocial who deviates from ethical values and to defend the nation and the dharma against external aggression. To serve the purpose, a second category of men emerged who were called the warriors (kṣatriya) and their leader, the king. The numerical expression 'second category', here is not intended to place the category at a level, lower to the first, in societal status. Every category of occupation serves an essential purpose of the society. Intellectuals, manual workers, businessmen and warriors, none is more or less useful for the society. The learned brāhmaṇa searches for truth and ethical values. The warrior implements and administers them, removing impediments and deviations, if necessary, by applying force through the authority of the state. Any one of the said four categories can function only with the active support of the remaining three. Indra is upheld as the ideal warrior to demonstrate the appropriate duties of the warrior and to inculcate self-confidence in him. Indra, the wielder of the thunderbolt is therefore, the first to be invited to a sacrificial function and the first to be offered the consecrated soma-juice by the sage, through melodious full-throated chanting of Vedic hymns. We will refer to some of these hymns later in this chapter. By simply remembering Indra, the wielder of the invincible thunderbolt, the warriors generate firm self-confidence, enough to win any war.

The wards of the warriors, like those of the brāhmaṇas and vaiśyas, were also admitted into the teacher's hermitage, to learn the Vedas, epistemology as well as the art and skill of warfare. Wars were fought mostly manually and weapons, if any, were to be operated by hand. This calls for ample physical strength of the arm. It is thus obvious that the kṣatriya is said to represent the arm of the society (*puruṣa*). He rightly belongs to the army. Arm here does not mean a limb of the physical body of any one. It only symbolizes the function of the warrior like that of the speech-organ symbolizing the intellectual (brāhmaṇa). The kṣatriya was also leading a married family life after graduation from the teacher's hermitage.

Similarly, the third occupational category of people are the (vaiśyas) businessmen. The commercial and financial aspects of the society are looked after by these people. They represent the thighs of the societal person (*puruṣa*), indicating that they have to frequently tour away to far off lands for their commercial activities. Not that they were always walking all the way. They were using vehicles and animals for transport. During these tours they were likely to be attacked by thugs and swindlers. There was therefore a convention that on the eve of the commencement of their journey they were offering oblations to sacrificial fire praying for a safe journey, for a profitable trade and for a safe return with enough wealth. They were also requesting the villagers to look after their homes and home-mates during their absence. They were collecting, carrying and selling the surplus merchandise of their area to consumers of far off lands where these are scarce and were carrying back home the surplus goods of those lands for sale. The transactions were frequently through barter. Occasionally gold was also used as a medium of exchange. The merchant (vaiśya) is no more or less important a limb of the society than the intellectual and the warrior. The children of the merchants also attend the teacher's hermitage to learn the Vedas as well as the basic principles of ethical trade and commerce. They are therefore, of the same type as intellectuals (brāhmaṇas) and warriors (kṣatriyas), born for a second time (*dvija*) to the societal world, on account of their graduation from the teacher's hermitage. On account of biological birth man is not different from a beast. One takes a second birth on acquiring a societal culture during the course of one's graduation. One becomes an expert (*vipra*) on the Vedas having deeply studied the Vedas. One who takes a vow to fully realize the implications of the Vedas, which is a lifelong exercise, and to spread the Vedic mantras by teaching these to others, another lifelong exercise, and constantly works accordingly, gets designated as an intellectual (brāhmaṇa). We have stated this earlier. In contrast, the merchant (vaiśya) engages in trade, commerce and industry. They also manufacture cars, bows, sacrificial posts and platforms etc., and presumably also agro-implements. They engage in a variety of manufacturing activities.

The next category, the śūdra, it is said, represents the legs of the societal person (*puruṣa*), i.e., he is engaged in manual work. He does not study the Vedas and is not initiated thereto (*upanayana*) by the teacher. He does not attend to direct sacrificial actions (*ayajvan*). He does not function as the priest who recites Ṛgvedic mantras (*hotā*) nor as the singer of Sāmavedic verses (*udgātā*). He also does not work as a Yajurvedic priest (*adhvaryu*) authorized to measure the sacrificial ground, to build the altar, to fetch wood and water etc., and to light the fire and to attend to other similar technicalities; nor does he work as a priest in general (*brahmā*). But he is available nearby to attend to all manual works. When invited they come in groups and lend their hundreds and thousands of hands for agricultural work against nine-sixteenth of the produce as their wages. They are experts in ploughing, planting and harvesting, acknowledge some Veda-mantras. As they thus provide the sustenance for the rest of the society, they are accorded full societal status equal with brāhmaṇas, kṣatriyas and vaiśyas. They do not come to render their services unless properly invited at their residences. As they are not trained by the teacher in any of the aforesaid sacrificial functions, they cannot adopt those occupations. They have enough physical strength and are experts in agro-activities. They are honourably eulogized. Keeping their equal societal status in view, some Veda-mantras enumerate the name 'śūdra' before that of the vaiśya.

The following are our renderings of some of the Veda-mantras in support of our views.

OBEISANCES TO AŚVINAU (Ṛk.8.35, sage, Śyāvāśva) (Translator's Note: Aśvinau: The twin heavenly physicians. According to Yāska they represent the transition from darkness to light, when the intermingling of both produces that inseparable duality expressed by the twin nature of these luminaries.)

"Come here to our sacrificial site O! The twin sons (of the Sun and the mare). Come with Mitra, Varuṇa, Dharma and the Maruts, your friends. Come O! also with Uṣas, Āditya and the Sun; Come close to our singing obeisances."

"Come hither, along with Aṅgira, Viṣṇu, Maruts and with all your powers, O! powerful Aśvins".

"Enliven our skill to know and arouse our intellect. Drive away our enemies and our ailments. Come along with Uṣas and the Sun and accept our offering, this soma-juice".

"Reinforce our protective forces, arouse our bravery and give enough milk to our cows to facilitate robust health of our people".

These verses high-light that fire is lighted in each home in the early morning so that one can offer ghee to it as well as can cook one's food. Since these functions are performed in each home, the twins are invited to each home. Fire generates heat and enough oxygen when ghee is burnt. Heat is also a disinfectant to facilitate good health. The twins are therefore described as the heavenly physicians.

THE VERSE TO THE BRĀHMAṆA, THE LEADING INTELLECTUAL (Atharva, 7.105, sage, Atharvan)

"Go ahead beyond the human limit choosing the light of language. Along with your friends, establish your societal lead".

"O, Aśvinī, the auspicious twins! saturate my words with the sweetness from the honey-bee; enable me to explain the profound voice of the Vedas".

"Bless me, O' Fire and Earth! O' Air and Fire! O' Āditya and the Heavens! O' Water and Varuṇa! Let the seven houses and the eighth that are capable of uniting all that is alive, bless us to complete our path and our project, so that I will succeed in explaining the blissful Vedic voice to all, the brāhmaṇas, the kṣatriyas, the vaiśyas, the śūdras and all else". [AN: It occurs to us that the seven houses are the progenies of the seven Vedic sages and the eighth is the council (*vidatha*) of the wise.]

"Let me measure up to my teacher's expectations. He gives me light and the girdle".

These verses are addressed to brāhmaṇas, sages and wise-men engaged in expansion of intellect, asking them to lead the society along the path of light.

THE VERSE TO THE KṢATRIYA, HYMNS TO INDRA (Ṛk.6.24).

"Indra's prowess glory and fame spread far and wide with *soma*. He is the most powerful. He sips fresh *soma*-juice. People offer obeisances to him singing of his glorious achievements. He is the emperor of songs. The heavenly Indra extends continuous assistances to men at all times."

"A wise friend of man, Indra's heroism has no parallel. He renders far-reaching help and support to those who sing his obeisances. He supports the poets.

He empowers those who offer him poetic obeisances in scholarly councils".

"O' great heroic Indra! Thou excel in excellence in both the heaven and earth, even as the axle in a wheel. Thou art honoured by all. Let thy numberless contributions to us proliferate, even as the branches and sub-branches of a tree".

"O' glorious omnipotent Indra! Let thy limit-less help come to us covering the whole of the path even as the cows cover the whole path while returning home. Our attachment to you is no bondage. It is like the calf's bondage to the cow".

"Indra fulfills all our wants one by one, from day to day, making explicit what was implicit. The gentle Indra, along with Mitra, Varuṇa and Pūṣan is ever prepared to bestow on us all that we ask for".

"Pleasing thee by songs and sacrifices, O' Indra! the poets make all the wealth from you flow to us freely, as if the spring from the hill-top. Thou art knowledge, i.e., Veda. Singing sweet songs, the poets approach thee, even as the horses approach the war, to arouse thy virility and strength".

"Indra does not grow old year after year. He does not tire after days and months. Let his youth stay intact for ever and his greatness and glory grow more and more, inspired by our eulogies and obeisances".

"We offer our obeisances to that light (*devatā*) the Indra who never bows down before his enemies, whatever be the might of the latter's muscles and minds".

"O' Indra! The Lord of our obeisances! The consumer of fresh soma-juice! Give us robust harvest and strength, stay close to us forever to help us, be extremely munificent during the dawn at the end of the nocturnal darkness".

"Keep close to our commander in war to save him from aggression from far and near, to save him ever from internal and external enemies. Let us live happily over hundred winters along with our heroic sons".

These are the Vedic verses in honour of the kṣatriyas. Indra is symbolic of the commanders and the fighters. In their mission to defend the society they can fight wars with equal ease, be it on the plains, on the hill tops or in the seas.

THE VERSE TO THE VAIŚYA AND ECONOMIC ORDER (Atharva 3.15, sage Atharvā)

"I am a trader. I invite Indra to come to us to lead us along the right path. Let him drive away the barbarians, the bandits, the docoits and the violent beasts from our path. He has no parallel in valiance. Let him help us to earn our wealth".

"Let me collect milk and butter from countless directions between the heaven and the earth. Let me create wealth by selling my collections".

Ṛk. 3.18.3.

"Offering ghee and fire-wood, I invite thee O' the light of the fire (*agni-devatā*)! I offer these oblations for my prosperity and strength. Chanting this mantra, singing these sacred verses to the best of my skill, I seek thy support to create hundreds of wealth".

"Pardon us O' Fire! for our tenacity for long tours. Permit us to profit from our purchases, sales and barters. Please accept our oblations. Let our long tours succeed".

"Let my investment grow without any loss. Accept O' Fire! my oblations, carry these to the other dignitaries as well, and let them and thee be pleased to frustrate any obstacle to our profit".

"Let my investment succeed in earning profits due to the blessings of Indra, Prajāpati, Soma and Fire".

"Accept our eulogies O' Vaiśvānara! Protect our kins, cattles and lives".

"O' Fire, the simple-awareness (*sarvajña*)! We stand, ever firm, as horses, beside (*upāsanā*) thee. Full of food and wealth, we shall ever invite you with pleasure. O' Light of Fire! Let us not suffer the pangs of poverty, being ever in your view".

To improve one's lot by one's own drive and self-confidence, the Vedic vaiśya involves light (*devatā*) by offering oblations to fire. One is grateful to fire that ensures safety of one's journey during the darkness of night.

THE VERSE TO THE ŚŪDRA AND TO AGRONOMY (Ṛk.4.57.)

"It is our friend, the Field Person (*kṣetra-puruṣa*), who helps us with our food-grains, the source of our sustenance and that of our domestic animals, cattles. Be he ever helpful to us in this regard".

"With your blessings, O' Master of the field (*kṣetra-pati*)! Let sweet water flow to our field, even as milk flows from a cow. Water is ghee for the crop. Shower your compassion on us O' maker of ghee (*ghṛta-pati*)!"

"Let water and herbs be honey to us. Let the breeze from the sky be honey to us. Let the Field Person shower honey. While following his foot-prints let us not bruise our feet".

"Let the bullocks, and the plough-men work with pleasant convenience. Let the plough have a free flow. Let the furrows be deep and close. Let the plough-bullocks be guided conveniently".

"Delight in our eulogies, O' Indra (*Śunāsīra*)! Please pour down on our earth the water you have in the heavens".

"Be close to each other, O' Furrows (*Sīte*)! We honour thee. Have compassion on us. Beget grains".

"Give company to the furrow (*Sītā*), O' Indra! Give her light, warmth and direction, O' Pūṣan (the Sun)! Let her be full of milk and gifts (grains) to us year after year".

"Let the plough function freely. Let the bullocks and the ploughmen proceed ahead without any obstacle. Let the clouds shower honey. Grant enough to us, O' Indra (*Śunāsīra*)!" (Even now the agriculturist in non-irrigated lands exclaims, 'It rains honey', seeing a suitable shower.)

It is clear from the following 'Ode to harvesting' that the aforesaid 'Field-person' and the 'plough-men' are śūdras. The Field-person, it is said, comes with hundreds of hands and heads, i.e., they come in groups to irrigate and cultivate. Thus the 'thousand-headed person' is not a Creator God; it is a group of men, the mankind in general. It concurs with my interpretation of the word '*Puruṣa*' in 'The Verse to the Person' (Ch.V).

THE ODE TO HARVESTING (Atharva, 3.24)

"The bushes are honey. My words are honey as well. Let me prosper with things (*padārtha* = meaning of a word in use) of honey".

"He is honey, I know. They had a bumper harvest. Let us invite, with due honour, the agricultural worker from the houses of those who do not perform sacrificial rites (i.e., śūdras). People of five professions from five directions bring us all our wealth, even as flood waters bring us timbers from hills and forests".

"Water from one spring flows down in a thousand channels. Let one piece of land grow grains thousand-fold".

"O' the hundred-handed (*puruṣa*)! cut, bundle up and bring the ripe grain bushes. Harvest and pour out the grains with your thousands of hands. Carry and heap together all these ripe grain-bushes, cut or yet to be cut".

"Three parts go to the king. The owner and his wife get four. The rest of the huge quantity is yours".

"Who harvest and heap up ripe grains are your two companions, O' Prajāpati (householder)! They bring you measure-less grains and seeds".

A person with a thousand hands, here, is obliviously a group of men working together with a single purpose, to drain in water to the field and to grow, reap and harvest plenty of grains. So '*Puruṣa*' is a group of men working with a single mind and objective. Living together in a group, men can facilitate progress, can coordinate and organize knowledge, can evolve expressive linguistic usages, can build up educational institutions, can organize better defence and can create plenty of wealth. Individuals are called upon to be determined to consciously work for progressive societal well-being. Group-life, cooperative farming, coordinated social life, academic excellence, trade, commerce and industry, defence mechanisms, all these and more become effective when individuals work with a firm commitment to the group. An individual has to sacrifice his narrow self-interest and has to take a vow to always work for the welfare of the group. All the Vedic verses exhort men to take such vows by lighting sacrificial fire. The system is designed as an effective coordinating mechanism. The body of knowledge that discusses this great truth from all angles in detail, and places it on a firm footing is called The Vedas.

Chapter VII

Family Life, Life in Peace and in War During the *Saṁhitā* Age

(1) INSTITUTIONS OF MARRIAGE AND FAMILY LIFE

Young boys and girls could enter family life only when the venerable teacher commands them to do so on completion of their education in the teacher's residential school, having lived there for 12 years or more and having achieved complete self-control over their bodies and minds, under strict supervision and discipline of the teacher and his wife. They then return to their parents, get married and lead conjugal life. One lives at home along with one's parents, brothers, sisters and wife with one heart and soul. One works to earn, lives an orderly coordinated life, caring for one's children and being kindly to the domestic animals. All members of the family congregate every morning and evening around the fire installed at home, and chant Veda-mantras. Tongues of all are sweet to each other. They are free from jealousy and hatred. The house-wife enforces discipline. The rest of the members are compliant. There is enough ghee, milk, honey, curd and food grains for all. The ideal leaders and dignitaries of the Vedic society could foresee for the first time in human history, and had taught accordingly, that it was advantageous for people to raise homes and to live a family life where each member was cordial to the others. The house was supported by strong pillars and was covered by thatched or reinforced roof. It was strong enough to thwart attempts of bandits, say some mantras. The house-wife was the empress of the family. Each member is subject to her discipline. There was usually one wife for one husband. Young widows and widowers were allowed to marry again. But they were determined to live for hundred years so that no one may suffer premature death. They were also determined to live an efficient life free from wants, ever alert to disband poverty, diseases and bandits. Their sense of aesthetics made the males, females and children to decorate their bodies with a variety of ornaments.

The sage pronounces in some mantras that a young widow can marry again a husband of her choice, and can be a proud mother of her brilliant children. Women are accorded very high honour and status, during the Vedic age, commensurate with their Vedic studies and the consequent intellectual acumen achieved during their days in the teacher's residential school, under the strict and stern supervision of the teacher's wife. They are equal with men in this regard. Learned and thoughtful girls are capable of selecting their husbands. This lady is fully empowered to manage her husband's household. Like an empress, she enforces discipline at home. Her husband's parents, brothers, sisters and her own children happily abide by such discipline. She always participates in her husband's rituals. No ritual is complete without her participation. Although introduced in the Vedic age, this custom is current even today. As she is well educated, she is invited, after gathering expertise in household management, to deliver talks to wise-men, in academic seminars. As said earlier, many ladies have displayed wisdom and have authored Veda-mantras. The house-wife is her husband's friend and companion during his youth and post-youth, and is as his mother when he is too old. A hard life attending to all household chores, keeps herself active over a long period, so that she is active even as a mother to her old husband. One mantra says that male and female dignitaries come to bless and encourage her when she is tired and perched on a couch, fatigued after a hard day of efficient house-hold chores. (Translator's Note: Approving and disapproving enlightenments emerge to replenish her spirits). Her loving and clear tongue to all the family-members facilitates the latter's loyalty to her and impels them to use similar tone and tenor among themselves.

The house-wife was equally kind and considerate to the domestic animals. The house of a good house-wife had enough number of vessels always full of milk, curd, ghee and honey. The children and the grown up young boys and girls had strong, shining bodies and the warriors were rugged and courageous, consuming enough of these. Some mantras clearly indicate that the house-wife is called upon to ensure that the domestic cattle get enough pure potable water. Similarly, the society is also called upon to ensure enough grazing grounds for these cattle. It is further indicated that the society was also kind to some non-domestic beasts and birds, as much as to the domestic ones. They were appreciative of the physical strength and of the beauty of the well-formed muscles of the tiger and desired that their young boys and girls display similar strength and beauty. They were also impressed with the great generative power of the Ox. Later, this power became personified as Lord Śiva whose emblem was the *Śiva-Liṅga* and who was always accompanied by an ox.

On graduation, while leaving the residential school (*gurukula*) the young man is called upon to carry to and install at home, fire from the sacrificial altar of the teacher. This fire has to be kept burning as long as the man lives and has to be finally used to consume his mortal remains. All family members, young and old, are to congregate around this fire every morning and evening and to sing the eulogies of the Vedic dignitaries. This rite is called '*Homa* (sacrificial offering)'. Fire, here, is symbolic of coordination of the members. This congregation, twice a day, fosters love and affection among them. Thus, the home, it is said, is the most sacred gift from the dignitaries.

While most young men and women adopt a house-holder's life, on completion of education, some of them choose to raise their own residential schools and to live there for life, each along with the spouse, teaching and learning. When they grow old, they no more shave. So they have long hairs. They then travel from village to village to educate the house-holders. They have no settled residence. They often live in forests as well. They are called the haired ones (*keśin*), the thinkers (*muni*) or the travellers (*paribrājaka*). They had clothing of golden colour (*gairika* = literally, 'of a hill'). The house-holders welcome them to their homes to live there for some time. They were travelling from this sea-shore to the other, travelling in the paths of the nymphs and *gandharvas* (singers). Their thoughts are firm and settled. They are engaged in doing good to the society at large.

The Vedas accord the girl a right to choose her husband. She likes to choose a husband who is bountiful, beautiful and erudite. So long as the girl is with her parents, *Aryaman* (Translator's Note: The Head of the manes, indicating societal care) takes her care. Mediators came to present to the girl proposals with briefs and biodata of prospective grooms. On one of the proposals being approved by the girl, it is gladly accepted by her parents. Then follow crowded marriage rituals and festivities during days and nights in broad sunlight and moonlight. Unmarried girls offer wholehearted cooperation for smooth completion of the function. After marriage, the bride proceeds to the groom's home in a procession accompanied by horses and cars loaded with articles of immediate use. The bride's villagers offer prayers (*vandāpanā*) wishing well of the couple. They also follow the procession up to a distance before they finally see them off. Then the procession proceeds from village to village taking care to avoid chances of bandits on unpopulated routes.

Seniors come to see her with gifts and blessings soon after she enters her new home. Then the couple take a vow, in front of fire that they will live together forever and that neither shall as much as even think of any other person of the opposite sex.

After practical experience of household management and on achieving a measure of maturity in the field, she is called upon to address academic councils of wise persons (*vidatha*) to deliberate on the desirable practices and policies that can be most suitable for effective and efficient management and maintenance of the institution of family. As a result, not only she earns recognition from wise persons, but new dimensions of house-hold management come to light. A well-done household management, it is said, leads the house-wife to intellectual (*para-loka*) enlightenment (*deva-loka*). As already indicated, the work is so arduous that the dignitaries come down to enthuse her when the tired house-wife retires to her couch after a hard day's work. (Translator's Note: Enlightenments emerge to replenish her spirits.)

Sūryā describes of her own marriage in symbolic expressions. Other unmarried girls speak to *Aryaman* about their choices on marriage. Once a proposal is settled the other suitors are asked to leave the place and to go to present themselves before other unmarried girls.

Incidentally, this healthy convention later developed to the system of *svayaṁvara* (own choice) where the maid chooses her husband. But the system soon got distorted. In Rāmāyaṇa it was not Sītā who chose her husband. It was Janaka, her father, who laid down the criterion that to qualify to marry Sītā one has to operate the old bow of Śiva (which eventually broke down in the hands of Rāma). But we desist from the digression here.

The following are our version (in *Oḍiā*) of the Veda verses that are the sources of our ideas.

Pativedana Sūkta, criteria to select a groom suitable for an effective married life, Atharva, 2.36, Sage, Pativedana.

1. "Let O' Fire! The young man desirous of marriage, select this maid and earn our friendship. Let the mediator be happy. Let this sparkling young lady, the beauty of this congregation, gain all the good fortunes along with her husband".
2. "Soma, the mantras sung by the Brahmā, all are fond of truth. By the force of truth and with the blessings of the cultured, I shall propose a suitable groom appropriate for this young bride".
3. "Let this lovable lady get a good husband, O' Light of Fire! She will then be blessed with a happy life by the king Soma. Let her be the empress of her home and beget worthy offspring. Along with her husband let this fortunate girl manage her family with ease".
4. "O' fortunate girl! Your groom shall always come back to you with love, even as a bird instinctively

comes back to its nest. Let there be no diversity between the couple".

5. "May all the wealth of the world carry you, smooth like a boat, to the groom of your choice".
6. "O' Lord of wealth! Impel her choicest groom towards this girl".
7. "Let this gold, this fragrant resin (*guggula*), this perfumed ointment and all these other auspicious articles impel your chosen groom towards you".
8. "Let the light of *Savitṛ* guide you to the groom of your choice. Grant this girl the skill to attract and to infatuate, O' herbs and plants!"

Marriage of Sūryā

Sage Sūryā speaks of her own marriage in the following words, Ṛk.10.85.

Felicitations to Soma

"Truth holds the world firm. The Sun describes the sky. Order (*ṛta*) upholds the Ādityas, as well as the Soma, well-placed in the heavens ... Someone may believe that he has drunk the juice extracted from a soma plant. But no one can ever drink the soma that has been realized by those who know the meaning of the Veda ... The Ādityas are rich with Soma. The world is firmly held together by Soma. Soma permeates the whole universe from the earth to the heavens".

Marriage Procession

"*Raibhi* was her friend. *Narāśaṁsī* was her companion on her way to her groom's home. Her bridal costume was sparkling with *Gāthā* songs". [Author's Note: *Raibhi, Narāśaṁsī* and *Gāthā* are names of metres of Veda-mantras. This verse indicates that the mantras to consecrate the marriage were sung using these metres.]

"Soma is the mediator to propose the marriage to Sūryā. The two Aśvinīkumārs, the effective mediators from the groom's side are also present. In these circumstances the light of *Savitṛ* handed to Sūryā the hand of the groom of her heart's choice".

"The procession organized by *Savitṛ* proceeds gracefully ahead. Cows are taken to the moon's mansion where the bride is given in marriage". (Translator's Note: The idea seems to be either that cows were presented to the couple at the time of marriage or that the marriage was consecrated at an auspicious time ruled by appropriate stars, i.e., cows.)

"Sit, O' Sūryā! In the car made of *kiṁśuka* (Translator's Note: A kind of tree having beautiful red blossoms) and *śālmalī* (Translator's Note: A silk cotton tree). The smooth glide of its wheels are auspicious. The car is beautifully decorated in various soothing colours. Let this journey to your groom's home be pleasant and auspicious. May this procession lead you to a life of beatitude".

Sūryā Enters Conjugal Life

"We devoutly worship you O' honourable Viśvāvasu! Let this maiden go with her groom. (Author's Note: Viśvāvasu is the name of a demi-god who provides security to an unmarried maiden.) (Translator's Note: It is stated earlier that the society protects the unmarried girl. The demi-god here appears to represent this societal force.) You may now take charge of the security of another unmarried girl going to reach her puberty".

"Let there be no obstacle on the path of our friends proceeding to the bride with marriage proposals. Let both Aryaman and Bhaga lead us along the right path. Let the lights ensure auspicious success of the marriage".

"I untie the girdle that was like Varuṇa's noose, symbolic of your virginity. The girdle was tied by the light that is *Savitṛ*, your well-wisher. (Author's Note: Unmarried girls used to put on a girdle as a symbol of their vow of virginity.) In the house of order (*ṛta*) and in the auspicious interest of the society, I unite you with your groom, free from all obstacles".

"I free you from here but not from there. I tie the nuptial tie tight. O' Indra, the bestower of wealth! Let this maiden be fortunate with her worthy offspring in her conjugal home".

"Let Pūṣan lead you from here by holding your hand. Let the twin sons of Aśvinī carry you in their car to the home of your groom. Be the empress of your new home, O' house-wife! You will later deliver your wise talk in the council of wise persons (*vidatha*)".

"Let your affection towards your children intensify. Be careful to manage your home with regular orderliness, cooperate fully with your husband in this regard. On achieving enough expertise in house-hold management you will be entitled in mature age to address the council of the wise".

"Let the couple escape bandits scheming to attack in the way. Proceed along a safe route keeping away from obstacles. Let the bandits run away from your route, in fear of their life".

"All the manners and demeanours of the bride are auspicious. Let everyone bless her for a happy and prosperous life. I take your hand for good fortune. I am your groom. Come and join me for life. Aryaman, Bhaga, Savitṛ, Puraṅdhi and other dignitaries have graciously granted me you to rule my home".

"Fire has granted him a brilliant bride of long life. Let the groom live long for a hundred autumns".

"Soma entrusted this Sūryā to a Gandharva (a demi-god) who handed her to Fire who now grants her to me along with wealth and worthy progenies".

Words of Blessings

"Be together for life. Let no one part. Play happily with children and grandchildren. Enjoy conjugal life at all times".

"Let Prajāpati grant you children. Let Aryaman keep you together even when you are old. Let inauspiciousness keep away from you both. Be kind to the bipeds and quadrupeds".

"Grant all wealth and maternity of worthy offspring to this dame, O' Gratuitous Indra! Let her beget ten children to make up eleven with her groom".

"Be the empress to your groom's parents, sisters and brothers".

"Let the lights of the world (*viśvedevāḥ*) and of waters stich our hearts in one bond. Let our breaths (*mātariśvan*), our bodies (*dhātrī*= lit. the earth) and our words that create knowledge (*jñāna-dātrī Sarasvatī*) bind us alike in one bond".

Atharva, 14.2.

"Be thy mornings brilliant with worthy children, with the home full of sweetness and with the cows yielding enough milk, when you wake up after fully enjoying your blissful bed".

Similarly, the Couple Address Each Other in Chapter 7 of Atharva Veda

The Groom Addresses the Bride

"Let our looks to each other be sweet. Let our countenances exude unity. Place me in your heart. Let our minds work as one".

The Bride Addresses the Groom

"I cover you with this my vest. Manu has gifted this vest. You are then mine alone. You will then cast no desiring look at another dame".

The Bride's Duties at the Groom's Home, Atharva, Ch.14

"Looking for good fortune, wealth, love and progeny, assist ever your husband in his profession. Keep ever awake towards these duties to deserve a life integrated (*amṛtatva*). I am your groom made so by Bṛhaspati. Be a proud mother to your worthy offspring and live with me for a century".

A Prayer for Smooth Completion of Marriage-Festivities, Atharva, 6.60

"This girl had worked hard to facilitate smooth completion of all the rituals and festivities in marriage of other girls. Let other girls similarly work hard towards a smooth completion of her marriage, O' mediator!"

Conjugal Life of the Couple, Ṛk.8.31.5 to 9

"O' Heavenly Lights! The couple jointly offer milk as oblation. They cooperate to grind soma juice and to wash (the grinder clean)".

"They collaborate in collecting food grains. They sit on mats of sacred grass (*kuśa*-mat). Their virilities are intact life-long".

"They do not divert from light (*devatā*), nor from the path shown by the enlightened. They earn immense glory for themselves."

"Generating worthy progenies and wearing gold ornaments they enjoy a normal happy life".

"Having invoked the lights (*devatā*) with elation, they jointly perform their conjugal dharma for the sake of an integrated (*amṛtatva*) life. Bonded together in love they contribute to enrichment of the glory of the enlightened dignitaries". [Author's Note: This means that the couple lives their conjugal life following the path shown by the enlightened (*devatā*). They decorate themselves with gold ornaments, are surrounded by their offspring and are bound together with the bond of love and live a full and ripe normal life in the usual manner.]

The Couple Raises a Residence, Ath. 3.12

"I place you here, O' sacred Home! Be safe and strong. With enough ghee etc., let our family live here a life of robust health".

"Stand firm sheltering our horses and cattle, ever full of food, milk, curd and butter, as well as, full of sweet, soft voices of the occupants. Be ever open to attract more and more wealth".

"Be a place of reassurance forever, standing with your tall roof, inside full of clean grains, O' sweet Home! Let the cattle with their calves return here every evening, spread out over the whole width of the path like a river when flooded".

"The dignitaries built you, O' my Home! You are the best bestower of compassion for us among all other houses around. Blessed be our heroic progenies and our ample wealth ever clasped to your bosom".

"Let the firm pillars and strong walls of this house continue to ever threaten the evil beings (*dasyu*). Let the inmates here enjoy a hundred autumns, free from any ailments."

"Here is the water that is clean and healthy. Here is the fire fuelled forever".

Service to the Mendicant, Ath. 15.11

"The householder must stand up and welcome a wise mendicant the moment he sees one. Asking him questions such as about his welfare last night etc., the former ought to offer water to the latter to wash his feet and to arrange for his meal as per his taste".

"The householder must honour and welcome the wise mendicant as he does towards his own seniors. He should leave no room for the mendicant to be annoyed with and to curse the householder or the state. It is the wisdom of the mendicant that is the source of all moral and statutory order".

(2) LIFE IN TIMES OF PEACE

People of Vedic culture are peace-abiding. They fully realize that progress and prosperity is possible, both for the society and for the state, only during peace time. Education, external and internal trade, agriculture, industry, all types of services and business can thrive only in peace. They wish to live, therefore, in peace, not only with men of other cultures but also with the whole of the animate world. Chapter 36 of Yajurveda proclaims as follows.

"I seek support from Ṛk (speech), Yajuḥ (mind), and Sāma (breath). I seek full peace by all means; in my faculty of vision, in my faculty of audition, in my faculty of speech and in each of my breath."

Let Bṛhaspati rectify all disorders, any narrowness, or any excess in any of these".

"I seek peace that reigns everywhere, the earth, the atmosphere, the sky, the vegetations and the waters. I seek peace that prevails in all dignitaries (*devatā*), all meanings (*padārtha*), meaning of meaning (brahma) and peace itself."

"Make me heroic O' Hero! Let all animals and men look up to me as a friend. Let me see all as my friends. Let us look at each other with loving eyes".

"Empower me O' Powerful! Let me live long with this urge at all times".

"Let us be fearless forever. Let our progenies prosper and our domestic animals remain safe and secured at all times".

"Be friends to us and foes to our foes, O' the World of vegetations and of waters!"

"Let us see the Sun a hundred autumns in the sky, the brilliant Sun that rises daily to shine like the sense of vision of the world. Let our faculties of audition, of vision and of speech, and their organs, work intact for a hundred autumns. Let our heads be held high for a hundred autumns. Let us live a robust life for even beyond a hundred autumns, if possible".

(3) LIFE IN TIMES OF WAR: MANTRAS ON WAR CHALLENGES AND WAR-DRUMS

Despite their devout desire for peace the Vedic *ārya* was ever alert to encourage and to inspire the poison-eating celibate youth to fight and win wars against aggressing enemies, barbarians and bandits. This we have already indicated while describing about poison-eating disciples (Ch.VI) and about Indra (Ch.IV and VI). The Vedas lay down that it was imperative for the whole of the population to unite and to work hard to feed and support the army and the commander at war time. Due to the influence of culture the aggressive instinct was kept under control during times of peace. It was therefore, necessary that anger was to be incited, aroused like a rage of fire, by means of beating of war-drums, says the Ṛgveda in the 'Verses to the rage of wrath' at Ṛk.10.84.

Verses on War-Challenges and War-Drums

(A) Verses to the Rage of Wrath (*Manyu sūkta*) and War Eulogy

"O' Rage of Wrath! Let our warriors with raised weapons, with sharp arrows, and seated on the war chariots, accompanied by you and by vital breath, charge towards the foe with fierce ferocity".

"O' Rage of Wrath! Win the war. O' Flame of Fire! Take the command of our warring army. Be the consecrated ghee, the oblation to our sacrificial fire.

Massacre our enemies, destroy their wherewithal, eliminate the aggressor with fierce force of your ire".

"Trample the aggressor beneath thy feet, O' Rage of Wrath! Charge ahead, crush, vanquish our enemy, burn and turn him to mere ashes kissing the earth. Nobody has ever withstood thy heroic prowess. You have come into being as the unbeatable master to subdue all".

"We worship thee as the only honourable light. Turn our army into an organized array of sharp weapons that destroy all. O' Flame unabated! We will hysterically encourage our army to follow thy foot-steps till they win the war".

"Grant us victory O' Rage of Wrath! You are invincible even as Indra, you are the Lord of all of us. At times of war we will enthusiastically sing songs of your glorious victory. We are aware of your place (Translator's Note: and time) of birth".

"We know that you are joined by Pūṣan in awareness. O' the Thunderbolt! O' the Destroyer! Your power to destroy is infinite. We will ever invite you in the midst of all fierce and ferocious wars. We know, you shall ever enthuse us."

"Let Wrath and Varuṇa join together to grant us double benefits. Let our foes be fully frustrated and flee back in our front".

(B) Verses to the Celibate's Vow to Fight and to Put on the Symbolic Girdle, Atharva, 6.133

1. "The Light (*devatā*) has made out and has tied this girdle around our waists. He has employed us in our

duties. We live at his command. He leads us out of any perilous path".

2. "We invoke you, we praise you, O' Girdle! You are the sage's weapon. Please accept our milk oblation and then devastate our fierce foes".

3. "I am the celibate of death. From among all the living creatures, I have chosen the Person (*Puruṣa* = AN: The class of warriors) for Death (Yama). I have carved the *Puruṣa* out through hard work, knowledge and penance. I tie him by this girdle".

4. "Grant us intellect and wisdom, grant us the powers of virility, self-control and penance, O' the Girdle! The daughter of trust and born of penance, you are the sister (Translator's Note: The Saṁskṛt word '*mekhalā*' is grammatically feminine) of the sage who ordains the world into order and truth, who builds up the beast into societal humanity".

5. "The sages who made the world, had you round their waists, O' Girdle! Stay tight around mine, so I may live long".

The idea here is to call upon the youth, at the time of investiture of the girdle, to stay ever determined to sacrifice the self for the sake of the society. Yama is the first to volunteer to die. He organized the world, it is said, into 'The World of the Manes (*pitṛloka*)', for men, and 'The World of Light (*devaloka*)' for the sages engaged in societal uplift. These sages initiate men into order and truth and call upon them to tie the symbolic girdle. Having tied the girdle, the celibate vows to work for human welfare and accordingly offers to march ahead to vanquish at the cost of his life, at war, the enemies of dharma and of culture. They are not afraid of death. Yama has taught them to lay down their lives while observing their duties. Thus, the cultured are peace-loving, but are ever prepared to effectively meet any war (Translator's Note: thrust upon them).

(C) Verses to the War-Drum, Atharva, 5.21

"Announce loud to our enemies, O' War-Drum! We shall make them mentally weak, distrustful among themselves, hate each other, disunited and fearful of each other".

"Let our enemies run away from the war-field, their minds, eyes and hearts inflicted with fear and unsteadiness, by the time we conclude our sacrifice".

"Made of hard timber and tightly fastened with thick leather, tanned with ghee, this Drum of ours inflicts instability and fear in the minds of our foes".

"With their minds numbed and trembling due to excess of fear, let our enemies run away from the war field at the frightful loud sound of our Drum even as wild beasts run away frightened at the sight of men".

"At the frightful loud sound of our Drum, let our enemies run away from the war field, bewildered and trembling with fear, even as goats and rams run away frightened at the sight of a wolf.

"At the frightening loud sound of our Drum, let our enemies run away from the war field, bewildered and trembling with fear even as birds fly away frightened at the sight of a hawk".

"Let our lights (*devatā*) that command the outcome of war, drive away our foes inflicting fear in their faculties, from the sound of our Drum tightly tied with tanned leather".

"Even though they have come well organized in aggressive formations they will retreat from the ferocious sounds of our Drums and from the piercing twangs of our bow-strings".

"Let your scorching heat inhibit the vision of our enemy, O' Sun! Let your scorching rays goad him away when the fire of his ire is already dimmed".

"O' Maruts, the progenies of Pṛśṇi! Thy prowess is powerful. Join Indra to eliminate our enemy".

"King Soma, Varuṇa, Mahādeva, Death and Indra, these our brilliant lights (*devatā*), will fight our war and will vanquish our foe".

As we have said, the celibates, inspired by their vows to fight to the finish, could invoke support from Indra to every time win wars against aggressors.

Chapter VIII

Approach Towards Decay and Vitality During the *Saṁhitā* Age

During the *Saṁhitā* Age the culture was fully realistic and humanistic. Fully aware of their situation, they were determined to widen the scope of life while facilitating human welfare. They were entirely optimistic. Their self-confidence knows no bounds. They knew that decay and death was bound to come but that could not make them dispirited or discouraged. They were ever alert and ever determined to usher in a fully active long life, free from ailments in a society of healthy traditions, despite the fact that individuals are mortal. After cremation of the deceased and after completion of the last obsequies they come back with a firm determination to live for a century or more. A young widow is advised by friends, relations and priests not to lament the dead but to return to the world of life, admitting a new groom to enjoy the warmth of life and to beget brave progenies. With a clear intellect and conscience, their determination to live a long, healthy and active life, free from wants due to human efforts and mutual collaboration, was unshakable till they depart. They were always wide awake to work for progress and promotion of life, drawing inspiration from the names of their predecessors who had become glorious deathless dignitaries by virtue of their self-propelled efforts towards societal uplift. Our *Oḍiā*-rendering of the following mantras will clearly demonstrate that the Vedic people used to return to active life with renewed determination after completion of the obsequies.

Verses to Rudra

"O' Ādityas! We are men. Death is our companion. Grant us a drive to work to prolong our lives" (Ṛgveda, 8.18.22).

"It is the three-eyed one (*Tryambaka*) that grants ripe flavor and nutrition. Let him detach me from the mortal life, like a ripe cucumber drops off from its stalk. Let him not detach me from a robust life, of immortal values" (Yajuḥ, 3.60). [Translator's Note: The verse expresses the universal aspiration of every one to live a normal life up to the age of full maturity. This entails that there should be no untimely death before it is naturally due. There is a variety of cucumbers (*Phutikākuḍi* = The cucumber that explodes when ripe), the thick skin on which cracks wide apart and it drops off from its mother stalk, all by itself, in its natural course, when it is ripe enough with nutritious food value emitting a soothing fragrance. The sage wishes that his thick-skin-like defining delimitation of primitive narrow, brutish selfishness be destroyed in its natural course, after he gains full maturity of his societal self, displaying his immortal societal worth of intellectual flavor and richness of societal value.]

"The discriminating faculty of someone may be a hundred times sharper than the average. But no one can surpass the order ordained by the enlightened dignitaries". (Author's Note: One must follow the foot-steps of Yama that one has to die.)

Verses to Rudra to Prevent Untimely Death, Yajuḥ, Ch.16, Sage, Parameṣṭhī

'O' Rudra! Shalutes to your wrath, to your sharp arrows and to your two mighty arms".

"Show me your auspicious form, O' compassionate Rudra! Keep us in your eyes of intimate blessings from the top of the mountain".

"Let your arrows from the top of the mountain fly in our favour. Do not destroy our men and animals, O' the Lord of the mountain!"

"We sing your auspicious eulogies and pray for happy and disease-free life for the whole of the living world, O' the Lord of the mountain!"

"Rudra is the first physician of the dignitaries. He pleads ever in our favour. He is our wise spokes-person. Subdue, O' Rudra! The snakes, and drive the evil spirits away to distant low-lying lands".

"Big or small, growing or grown up, kill no one, O' Rudra! Kill no one's parents, stroke not our bodies with your scorching rays".

"We hold you ever in our hearts, O' Rudra! Kill not our cattles, horses, our warriors, nor the flame of their fire of ire."

"O' Master of Soma-juice! People flee away from thee in fear. Threaten not our children, nor our domestic animals with the fear of destruction. Let none of us suffer from any ailment".

"The infinite source of all the price-less wealth and of all that is auspicious, O' Rudra! Be kind and loving to us. Come to us in your leather vest and with *pināka* in your hand (*'Pināka'* is the name of the bow that protects and inspires). Leave behind your other arms and ammunitions on a distant tree". (Author's Note: During noon time the sun itself is located on the top of the mountain. But it burns the world below almost into ashes with its scorching stroking heat. The sun however, is as well, the source of all the energy needed for birth, sustenance and growth of life. Its scorching rays disinfect, as well as cause the rains facilitating vegetations. Rudra thus displays these two features. The sage here is enamoured with the auspicious features.)

These verses speak of the infinite blessings of the scorching solar power that sustains the bio-environment. It destroys the harmful infectious germs and insects as well. Its light and heat is excessive when it is on the top of the mountain. It kills serpents, scorpions, reptiles etc., harmful to men. It is thus addressed as 'the jewel of a physician' (*Bhiṣak-ratna*). But excess of heat can also burn plants and vegetations, kill domestic animals and dry up water everywhere. Children can suffer untimely death due to sun-stroke. Warriors suffer quick exhaustion in war-fields. The sage sees this dual feature of Rudra. On the one hand it has many beneficial features, can generate healing forces and vital energy contributing to longevity, while on the other hand it can cause severe suffering and premature death due to excess of heat. The sage, therefore, sings these eulogies in praise of Rudra's beneficial aspects, praying him to keep away from his destructive dance of *tāṇḍava*. This Rudra is not the Śaṅkara of the later Purāṇa age. It may be noted, incidentally, that in Rāmāyaṇa Vālmikī brings in the story of Rāma breaking down the bow of Śiva, with a view to bring out the superiority of Viṣṇu over Śiva in his effort to re-establish Vedadharma. The description of Rudra in the foregoing Vedic verses appears to resemble that of Śiva of the later Purāṇa literature in many respects, but the name 'Śaṅkara' is not found in the Veda, although the Veda recounts eleven names of Rudra corresponding to his eleven forms. Vedic Rudra, thus, is not the same as Śaṅkara of the later ages.

Verses on the Last Rites, Ṛgveda, 10.18, Sage, Saṅkusuko

"Proceed along the path laid down for you, O' Death! Your path is entirely distinct from the one of the dignitaries (*devatā*). I speak to you because you can see and listen. Be not angry with our children and with our warriors in the war-fields".

"You may now turn back from the path of the dead. You have many miles to go, miles of abundance, miles of life, proceed. Grow with your progenies and with your wealth. Sacred, pure, enlightened be your life, comparable to those of the dignitaries".

"We have sent these people back from the path of the dead. Let the dignitaries bestow blessings on them. Dancing and enjoying, we proceed along the flow of life. We hold firm on to a long life of abundance".

"I have cordoned the living off. Let them not cross. Let them bury death beneath the mound of earth and then enjoy a hundred autumns abounding in pleasures and profits". (Author's Note: The dead body was buried/burnt and an earthen mound was raised thereon. This mound is honoured as the house of the deceased. That was their duty to the departed.)

"Let each one who is here be careful to live for the full span of his active life and later welcome old age, in course of time. Let Viśvakarmā, the ordainer of all welfare, be your friend and guide you to long lives".

"Let the ladies living with their husbands, wipe off their tears and anguish and lead the rest in returning back to home, having anointed their bodies with ungent and sandal-paste perfumed with camphor and ghee, and having been fully embellished with their choicest ornaments".

"Wake up O', charming young Lady! The man thou mournst is no more. Come back to the world, come back to the society. Start living as the wife of the man who holds your hand and intends to be your husband". (Author's Note: This verse indicates that a young widow can marry again.)

"Let us take over the bow from the dead. Let both of us enter into the societal stream vibrating with valiance and virility, right from here. Let us procreate promising progenies and earn victory over all our ill-wishers scheming to prevent and threaten us".

"Let this earthen mound stay soft over the dead and be his comfortable home of a thousand pieces of earth joined together".

"I have built this mound for you, around you. Let me suffer no loss as a result. Let the manes protect the mound. Let it be the Yama's palace for you".

"I was called upon to do this on the day this counter-event occurred. It was as if an arrow flies back-wards. I plead for the reverse order even as one reins in a horse back-wards".

"Subside and cool the place, O' flaring Fire! Let many plants and bushes grow with lush green leaves and *sadāvihārī* flowers (it flowers in all seasons)".

Verses to Yama, Ṛgveda, 10.13, Sage, Vivasvān

"In deference to the dignity of intellectual brilliance (*devatā*) he chooses disintegration (*mṛtyu*) for his own body of flesh. He chooses not, integrity (*amṛtatva*) for the mortal human body. The body of this wise sage is thus sacrificed as an oblation. As a result, Yama lays down his own biological body.

Ṛgveda, 10.14.

"Honour him with oblations. He is the son of *Vivasvat*, the one that heals. Yama has laid down the path for men, after very intense and painstaking search into many far-reaching consequences. The search was more arduous than climbing up many inaccessible tall mountains at very far off territories."

"Yama discovered, and thus leads us to, our final abode, the land that no one can snatch away from us. Your manes have gone there. Anyone who is born, himself adopts this path".

"Go and join your manes and Yama there. Fulfill all your aspirations in that land of the widest heavenly enlightenment. Live there in your body of light leaving away all your limitations".

"Pour down soma-juice and offer other oblations for Yama in the sacrificial fire. It is through fire that all sacrifices reach him".

"Offer libations of ghee standing beside the sacrificial fire. He will then beg for us long life from the dignitaries".

"Offer your most palatable oblations to king Yama. That amounts to your tribute of deep trust to the past path-makers, the sages".

Our *Oḍiā* rendering of these 'Verses on the Last Rites' and to Yama indicates that the rites were accomplished in two stages. An earthen mound was raised on the place of cremation. (Translator's Note: The relative *Oḍiā* expression, "*keteka mṛta-vyaktiṅku māṭigadātaḷe samādhi diāyāuthilā*", can also be translated as "Some dead-bodies were being placed beneath a tomb of an earthen mound".) They were praying Yama to protect the mound from wearing out. They were also dressing up the mound with grass with a view to prevent wearing out, so that it remained in place, as if it was a house built up by Yama for the departed. Where the dead-body was burnt, they wished the fire at the place of cremation to cool off. Even now there is a customary rite to cool the fire (Translator's Note: *Rohi-śītaḷa. Rohi = rayi = water*). Water is sprinkled on the ashes and a piece of bone is collected to be assigned to a river at a sacred place. This current rite is symbolic of the Vedic rituals. After the fire cools out they draw consolation from planting flower plants at the place. The plants draw their sustenance from the ashes of the dead. Death, thus, contributes to life. Vedic civilization consciously accepts death as a natural event. If the fresh widow is young she should accept a new groom, she is advised by the priest and by her friends and relatives. This custom is irrespective of whether an earthen mound is raised or the body is simply burnt. Some say, marriage of a widow was customary only among the warrior class (kṣatriya). We disagree. The Vedas clearly indicate that the custom was current among all the four professional classes, brāhmaṇa, kṣatriya, vaiśya and śūdra. The priest advises all the friends and relations of the deceased present at the funeral, to return to a normal healthy life of abundance. Let the deceased go in his path and let the others go ahead in the path of life full of happiness and wealth. Death and life run counter to each other. The priest indicates this when he says that he has cordoned the living off from the dead and that the living should now stop mourning and start returning back to normal life. Even now it is customary to draw a line across the path by an iron nail after the eleventh day obsequial offerings on the path (*patha-śrāddha*) and to prohibit the departed to cross the line back. The description of death as a counter-event, as if it was an arrow flying back-wards, is reflected in today's obsequial custom of measuring boiled paddy on a grass-mat etc., that amounts to seeing things and events in their reverse order. The current custom of wearing new cloth and feasting on the tenth day also reflects the Vedic verse where the ladies living with their husbands are asked to put on perfumery etc., and to lead the rest to return home with normal costumes and ornaments. Taking bath after the 10th day obsequies the relatives currently put on new cloths and visit the nearby temple where the males put on sandal-paste and the ladies dye their feet with red-resin (*alakta*). These customs also echo the obsequial practices of the Vedic age. The current practice of addressing the crow as the messenger of king Yama and asking it to carry the message to the latter, resounds the Vedic verses, "Yama discovered and thus leads us to our final abode ..." and "Proceed along the path laid down for you, O' Death! ..." Even now the priest sings, "one must die one day, why need one lament?" (*Tatra kā paridevanā*? Gītā, 2.28). These normal and natural responses to death, the vow to see and enjoy a hundred autumnal Suns and Moons, and to live a healthy life of vitality and abundance, speaks volumes about the approach of the Vedic sage towards life and vitality. This approach is in contrast with that of *Dharmabaka* (the crane that is Dharma) to death and life during the later Mahābhārata age. 'Daily some people die. Yet the rest wish to live forever. What is more astonishing?' asks *Dharmabaka* to Yudhiṣṭhira. This view amounts to discouraging life. Seeing a dead-body, *inter alia*, the young sentimental Gautama retired to the forest leaving behind the warmth of his cozy family life, undertook penance and finally preached the mantra of self-annihilation (*nirvāṇa*). These are approaches contrary to the Vedic traditions and are indicative of extraneous religious forces. [Translator's Note: *Dharmabaka* asks 'What is astonishing?' and the aforesaid statement was Yudhiṣṭhira's answer. Since *Dharmabaka* was satisfied with the answer, our author takes it to represent a general approach towards life during the post-Vedic period. The story about Gautama also implies that the Buddha preached no absolute annihilation but annihilation of a strictly private narrow self on acquisition of a greater and wider societal existence (*saṅghaṁ śaraṇaṁ gacchāmī*, I surrender to the society). Thus the author seems to highlight that any negative approach to life runs counter to the Vedic spirit]. Veda-dharma is entirely humanistic. The Vedas are determined to live a life of happiness and abundance. They ask us not to be overwhelmed at the idea of death. They exhort and encourage one to fully enjoy the warmth of life with self-control, with abundance of wealth and without any malady or sickness. We will reiterate this approach towards decay and vitality during the *Saṁhitā* Age, in the next Chapter, while discussing 'The Song to the Soil' of the Atharvaveda. The soft poetry, the sweet words and the profundity of thought of that song is so greatly appealing that one comes there across a comprehensive reflection of the whole range of the Vedic culture. The Vedas were very firmly determined to march forward with commitment to fully enjoy life, dancing, singing, with optimism, with boundless self-confidence, in keeping with the societal and ethical order. This culture preaches no aversion to wealth (*viṣaya-vairāgya*), no theory of creation (*sṛṣṭitattva*), no surrender at the feet of the Creator, no shrill shriek from the agonizing churning of the whirlpool of the world. There is no annihilation of 'Being' for the *Saṁhitā*. All the visible events and developments in the world are intelligible only with an assumption of this 'Being', the 'Golden-womb' that was ever pregnant with infinite possibilities. Dignitaries and men take birth. The former are resolute to lead the rest along a path of progress and prosperity. They are friends and predecessors of humankind. Indicating this, the Gītā pronounces that 'when analytically segregated from 'simple-being (*sat*)', 'Becoming (*asat*)', as a concept, has no existential (*bhāvaḥ*) implication (*nāsato vidyate bhāvaḥ*, Gītā, 2.16), and 'simple-being' is not conceivable apart from existential implication (*nābhāvo vidyate sataḥ, ibid*). With a view to reiterating Veda-dharma, Ācārya Śaṅkara comments that 'A discussion about creation is pointless'. (Ref. Translator's Note at Para.1, Ch.V). Any effort to locate the first cause is bound to prove futile. Uncategorized (*nirguṇa*) Brahman, i.e., indescribable (*anirvacanīya*) 'simple-existence' (*sattā*) is a-temporal. Even in the practical parlance, who can bring about anything from nothing? Where there is no fire, has anyone seen fire flaring up simply if someone commands, 'Let there be fire'? A hard brick can be manufactured by manipulating certain material components, earth, sand etc. Material components can be processed into new finished outcomes, but 'simple-existence' (*mauḷika sattā* = existence as such) cannot be brought about by any length of rigorous processing. What the sage of the *Saṁhitā* says, is reiterated by the Gītā and Ācārya Śaṅkara. 'Each time dharma degenerates I come back to reiterate', says Śrīkṛṣṇa of the Gītā, meaning that during various periods of history various sages and path-makers, like Manu, come forward to guide humanity. The Purāṇas also reiterate the point in a different style. They picture Viṣṇu as perched on a floating leaf in the vast ocean at the time of the primal dissolution, to indicate that 'simple-existence' is a-temporal. From Viṣṇu's navel-lotus emerges *Brahmā*, the architect of creation (*Prajāpati*), who then works out the whole world intact. This shows that when everything can dissolve, 'simple-existence' is indissoluble and forms the referential foundation of gradual emergence of all names and forms. The concept of a limit-less number of worlds emerging from each pore of thy skin (*Brahmāṇḍa māla māla hoi, to lomakūpe virājai, Oḍiā Bhāgavata*), similarly symbolizes the Vedic concept of the Golden-womb. Although during the Purāṇik age much filth and rubbish got interpolated into the Vedic thought, the basic structure of the latter, however, continues to work as the primal assumption of all Purāṇas.

The Veda-mantras, thus, record no commandment of a Creater God. They record the conclusions of various deliberating councils of wisemen concerning the possible *modus operandi* of life that can lead to pleasant and prosperous living. The Vedic *Saṁhitā* does not say, that a Supreme Creator initially created the world out of nothing, and then the living beings and men, that it was He alone that knows why He created men and in what lies man's welfare, and that it was man's best duty, therefore, to strictly abide by the God's express commandments. They do not say either that the God is willful and the world comes into being simply at His will or that a God-man condescended from the heavens to teach that men should tread the path shown by him so that the will of the willful God can be fulfilled. The *Saṁhitā* presents the sage's resolve to work for human welfare. The components of this concept of welfare are worked out in the following manner.

An individual is found to expire. Death cannot, therefore, be a cause to discourage life. Enjoy the full span of a long life and welcome death when it is due. Immature death is unnatural. With a firm resolve to prevent this, one is asked to work accordingly. One can live for a hundred or a hundred and twenty years of active life with full vitality, free from ailments, it is said. Accordingly, one is advised to adopt the following healthy practices. To start with, one should reside in a house built with strong pillars on a higher platform. Ensure uninterrupted supply of clean water and air. Procure and preserve enough food grains and water for men and domestics. Cereals must be supplemented with enough of milk, curd, ghee and honey for regular consumption of all family members. Fire and Sun are helpful to keep infection away. So all the family members must wake up before sunrise and congregate around fire after cleaning their bodies to resolve for the day's duties with cordiality towards each other. They should then engage in their respective professions such as cultivation etc., until the sun is too hot. The sweet cleanliness of the dawn, as also the light and the rays of the rising sun facilitate clarity of perception, of vision and of audition, contributive to knowledge and to efficient performance of professional functions. The Dawn and the Sun are thus eulogized in verses of welcome. Since excessive solar heat is harmful to human body, people are advised to keep away therefrom. Sunlight is welcome to the extent it disinfects and facilitates human activity. At nightfall people should offer libations to fire (in sacrifices), to light the house and to keep the harmful beasts and insects away. The ground and the neighbouring environ gets disinfected. Such sacrifices are, therefore, very useful, it is said. Traders, travelling from one village to another during night, can infer the directions from the lights of these sacrificial fires at human settlements, and can avoid attacks from bandits. The Veda-mantras tell the truth that human longevity can be prolonged by keeping the immediate surroundings disinfected. One should not distort the overall biosphere by careless killing of beasts and birds and by mindless felling of forests. Societal and ethical conduct creates human conscience. The sage prefers societal well-being to a narrow self-interest. A private individual strictly outside the society is an insensible imagination, pronounce the Vedas. What is good and what is not, can be distinguished only in knowledge. Knowledge is based on experience. Knowledge gains clarity and expression from use of language, possible only in the society. Societal interaction occasions use of language and that is possible only in a society where people need to exchange ideas through use of sentences. Exchange of ideas creates a greater and a more cohesive society, in the true sense of the term. Each individual is aware of his relativity to others. It is thus that use of language is at the root of all evolution. 'The Council of the Wise (*vidatha*)' used, by all means, to encourage each participant to achieve progressively greater and greater refinement of his skill of expressive use of language, through continuous debates and deliberations. It is repeated every now and then that private knowledge and private language was impossible. An individual cannot be expected to live a healthy life in an unhealthy society. It is clearly desired that each member must strive his best towards eradicating all societal evils and maladies.

To sum up, the Vedas exhort that the highest human goal (*parama-puruṣārtha*) lies only in a societal life of self-control with an abundance of joyous enjoyment based on creation of enough of wealth. The Vedas discourage any aversion to wealth. It is not enough merely to keep the body fit and active. One has to keep it beautiful and the mind blissful. Cleanliness for good health and ornaments and cosmetics for aesthetic beauty, both these dimensions have been clearly highlighted. Peace is desirable. It mothers all kinds of progress and prosperity. But for the sake of uninterrupted peace one has to fight with full force and finish the foe forever. This idea is also later reiterated by Śrīkṛṣṇa in the Gītā when he inspires Arjuna to resolve to fight. After the day's hard work to earn wealth and eatables, people are called upon to congregate at the Council Hall in the evening to enjoy music and dance. This Council Hall and its precincts is the place where people practice physical exercises for good health, learn use of various weapons to win wars and participate in debates and deliberations to enrich awareness. Influence of this Vedic culture can even now be traced to the current concept of Community Centres (*jāgāghara*) encouraging physical exercises in the mornings and music in the evenings. Performances of simple and appealing sacrificial functions in these precincts are designed to provide wide opportunities to people of all the four professions to work together to encourage societal cohesion. Since it was accepted that all developments emerge from societal living, the Vedic society accords equal societal status to all the four professional types. Having fully realized this truth the Vedic people lived in clusters of villages. They had also introduced the system of joint farming. They knew that it was convenient to canalize water for irrigation from far off springs, when many people join hands in large numbers. A large number of cultivators can raise and pool enough resources to pay for a decent wage to each of the numerous śūdras required to attend to all the multifarious manual works needed for effective agriculture. Economic and efficient processes can be conveniently adopted for cultivation in large fields. Services of a large number of manual workers are called for to till, irrigate, plant and harvest all the fields simultaneously. Aware of this, agriculturists from all the remaining three professional classes jointly visit the śūdras' village to invite the latter to work against wages. The śūdras are jointly designated as 'The Field Person' because they join together in cooperation to work in the field for a robust crop. Since people visit the śūdras' village and cordially invite them to work in the fields, the Vedas accord, at many places, to the śūdra, a societal status, higher than that to the vaiśyas. Through trading and commercial business of the crops, *inter alia*, the vaiśya generates his wealth mostly for his own consumption. But the crops produced by the śūdras through their collaborative group efforts, go to feed and sustain the whole of the society. For agricultural activities a large quantity of manual labour becomes absolutely necessary at a particular time.

Professional Labour has been clearly recognized, thus, as an inevitable component contributing to an overall societal well-being.

The Vedic society, thus, is free from wants, is free from any discriminatory allocation of a higher or a lower societal status to any segment, and is also free from any manual or mental malady. All-round and collaborative efforts prevail, victory in wars is ensured and life is pleasant and peaceful. These are the objectives of the Veda-mantras. Learned and wise sages render appropriate guidance to the dignitaries (*devatā*) engaged in society-building. These dignitaries are there not in the Heavens, away from men. They always accompany men constantly and tirelessly, working towards human welfare. Service to the roaming mendicant (*atithi*) helps eradicate malice from the society and reinforce societal cohesion, it is also clearly announced. The Vedas also specifically encourage one to offer food to one in need, to help the poor and to serve the ailing, by all means. The Vedic ideal is:

'Let all be happy and free from ailment,
Let all see excellence and no one lament'.
(*sarve bhavantu sukhinaḥ*
sarve santu nirāmayāḥ
sarve bhadrāṇi paśyantu
mā kaścit duḥkhabhāk bhavet.)

Chapter IX

The Song to the Soil (*Bhūmi Sūkta*) and Our Conclusions

While one has to remain ever prepared to subdue the adversary in war, at the cost of one's life, one has to participate, during peace time, for the sake of one's good health of both body and mind, not only in physical games and exercises, but also in dance, drama and music, in sacrificial rites, and in debates and discussions on Veda-mantras, in the Council Hall and its precincts. These ideas are again reiterated in 'The Song to the Soil' in the Atharva Veda. Peace is the objective. But to achieve this, war has to be fought, tooth and nail, if it becomes necessary. This Song is so appealing and is so saturated with so much of poetic beauty that I feel tempted to reproduce most of it here. The Vedic seer addresses and inspires the whole of the human race through the compelling force of his poetic grace. This sacred soil, the earth, answers to Indra, who not only ordains order, truth, resoluteness and initiation (*ṛta, satya, vrata, dīkṣā*) but also destroys *Vṛtra*, the one that violates these prime values. The poet envisages a world of men of a hundred hues of nationality, of culture, of languages, all living together in collaboration, in peace and in happiness. The Song is as sweet as profound. The first and the foremost poetic mansion in the whole history of human culture, it stands out as the tallest architecture that inspires humanism for all times to come. The tallest architecture is also studded all over with many pieces of sublime poetic art all of which are held together by the last piece of the top like the one on the top (*dadhi-nauti* = the topmost balancing piece of pitcher-shaped capital stone of a temple) of the sublime architecture of the tall temple at Koṇārka, placed by the expert architect, the legendary Dharmapada. (Translator's Note: On account of its commanding height of universal humanism, Verse 63, the last verse here, holds thc whole of the Song in place, saturated with humanistic richness and brilliance. For the same reason, the whole Song of 63 verses is also seen by the author as the apex poetic articulation that holds the entire Vedic literature in place. The allegory here is to the legendary young architect Dharmapada who, having quietly studied the science at home, accomplishes the task of placing with graceful ease, the topmost piece of balancing pitcher-shaped-capital stone on the tall temple Koṇārka in one go, even when the senior architects were still debating for long about the various ifs and buts of the matter.) The Song sings 63 verses some of which we reproduce.

The Song to the Soil, Atharva, 12.1. Sage, Atharvan

1. Truth is profound and stable. Dedication (*dīkṣā*), penance (*tapa*) and sacrifice (*yajña*) hold the world stable. It is this soil (*bhūmi*) that sustains like an empress, the past and the future. Let her widen our environ.

2. This is the soil that holds the hills, the slopes and the planes in place. Beauty is its creepers, its shrubs and its herbs. It is the joint habitat of men; it makes all the room for all of us.
3. This is the soil that is the store-house of the seas, of the rivers and of all the rest of the water-reserves; of the grains, of the granaries and of all the foliage that breathe life. Let it bestow its best blessings on us.
4. Like the house-wife to all the four quarters, she grows grains at the right time in the fields to sustain all that breathe. Let her grant us enough of eatables and domestic animals.
5. This is the soil where the manes worked in the past. It is here that the dignitaries destroy the demons. It supports the cattle, the horses and all the rest of the birds and beasts. Let her grant us all the riches, abundance and brilliance.
6. This soil, the earth is the best place for human habitation. It bears in its golden womb, all the minerals and all else that is valuable. It has light, warmth and blessings of Indra and Ṛṣabha.
7. All the dignitaries are ever awake, without any exception, to always support and sustain this soil, the earth. Let her grant us enough of palatable food for our glowing good health.
8. Land on this earth was initially submerged in water. Wise men searched it out with an unequalled insight. Timeless 'being' is at the heart of this earth, covered up in 'truth' and in

'integration (*amṛtatva*)'. Let her grant us physical virility and intellectual brilliance.

9. This is our earth where water flows all-round, enough for all, round the year. Let her also grant us milk flowing down like a river, for our handsome health.
10. Aśvinī takes its measurement. Viṣṇu circumscribes (*parikramā*) it. It is the same earth saved from the ugly hands of the enemies killed by the great valiant Indra. Let this glorious earth feed me with abundant milk, even as a mother.
11. Let thy hills, thy snow-clad-mountains and thy dense forests be pleasant O' Earth! with all the brilliant colours, catechu (*khaira*), black, red and others, ever protected by Indra. I am unslain, unhurt, and unsubdued on this earth.
12. Let me stand stout between thy centre and thy atmosphere, reinforced by thy life-giving vitality. Consecrate me from all angles. Thou art my mother, I am thy child. Rain is my father. Let the rain-cloud grant me an abundance of everything.
13. Thou art the support for the tall, glowing and strong pillars of our sacrificial platforms where libations can be offered and sacrificial threads spread out. The source and support of all evolution, bless us to evolve.
14. Those who hate us are hostile. They threaten us with waving weapons and with wicked intents. Subdue them, O' Earth! as you had done in the past.

15. Bipeds and quadrupeds spring up from and move around on thy bosom. Holdst thou them firm close to thy warm breast. Thou art the support for all the five types of men. The Sun rises daily to enlighten these mortals who spread out their tribes to all the four directions.
16. Let all those who live, unite to spread out all over, the springs of bliss and blessings. Grant, O' Earth! sweetness to my speech.
17. This is the earth that bears all these shrubs, creepers and trees, and is firmly upheld in place by order (*ṛta*). Let her graciously grant us an uninterrupted flow of wealth, as long as we tread her bosom. (Author's Note: It is indicated here that all the human happiness and wealth flow from a sustainable environmental equilibrium.)
18. Thou art our home, O' Earth! glorious and wide. Thy speed, thy throb and thy motion, all are glorious. The great heroic Indra errs not at all, in protecting thee forever. Sustain us at all times. Grant us a glitter of gold. Let no one despise us.
19. Warmth of fire (Author's Note: energy) resides in thy womb, in the trees and in all that lives. This flare of fire resides in stones and burns bright deep within the bodies of all the men, cattle and horses, as well.
20. It is the selfsame fire that resides in the sky, in the environment and is lighted in sacrificial rites for oblations and libations of ghee to be offered.

21. When I grope around in dark, let this earth enlighten me by the light of her fire, for my intellect to glitter like a sharpened sword.
22. People offer libations to the dignitaries in sacrifices on ornamented altars built up on thy soil. Thou art the seat for the mortals to eat, to drink and to live on. Grant us vitality and breath enough for a long life.
23. The fragrance thou hast injected into the trees and into the creepers, the fragrance that enchants even the demi-gods, let that fragrance, O' Earth! confer on me unprecedented melodious harmony (*apūrva mūrcchanā*).
24. The fragrance that penetrates the lotus, was first brought into being by the dignitaries, on the sacred occasion of Suryā's marriage. Grant me the same fragrance to sweeten me, O' Earth! Let no one see me with eyes of disregard.
25. That is thy fragrance that permeates the men and the women. It is thy lovely aura that sparkles on the bodies of men, warriors, horses, elephants and beasts. It fulfills the body of the young maid with beautiful reddish glamour. Infuse, O' Earth! all these in me in abundance.
26. Rocks, clays, boulders and dusts, all are well-coordinated in thee. I offer my hearty salutes to thee, the gold-bearing earth.
27. Welcome thee O' Earth! Thou holdst together firm, all the foliage of small plants and large trees, all the waters and lands, and all the rest that lives.

28. Hold us ever firm and stable, O' Earth! when we sit down, when we rise up, when we remain standing or when we walk about. (Author's Note: Let us suffer no infirmities.)
32. East, West, North or South, let us not miss any of the directions, O' Earth! Save us from the imposters misguiding pedestrians into wrong paths to swindle them. Keep us away from our deadly weapons in our normal life.
35. Let all I extract from thy bosom, get quickly replenished. Let us not destroy, even by mistake, thy life-sustaining potency, O' consecrating Earth! Let us not tear thy bosom apart.
36. A year's time is built up of your seasons, O' Earth! the summer, the rains, the autumn, the mild winter, the chill winter and the spring. Let all your seasons, the days and the nights grant us abundance.
37. The earth consecrates all, drives the snakes away for our safety, its warmth penetrates the waters as well. The earth subordinates itself to Indra and not to *Vṛtra*. The earth destroys the swindlers who dislike our dignitaries. It is this earth that keeps its valiant valour ever embraced to its bosom.
40. Let all the wealth we need, be ours on this earth. Let the brillinance (*bhaga*) of excellence (*aiśvarya*) keep us engaged in our duties. Let Indra lead us along the right path.

41. It is on this earth that men sing, dance and enjoy. It is also here that they engage in bitter fights with loud cries and war-drums. Drive our enemy far and farther away, O' Earth! Keep us free of enemies.
43. It is here that the grains grow; paddy, malt, barley etc. It is here that live people of five cultures. We bow down to this earth. Let the water that flows to sustain vegetation, keep her wet and cool.
44. Let all the gems, pearls, gold and diamond, held hidden, all over the earth's bosom, be ours. Let the mother earth happily and heartily grant us an abundance of wealth (*vasu*).
45. It is on this earth that people evolve and use a variety of languages and of ethical codes (*dharma*) at different regions. Let resources flow to us in various channels from her, even as milk from a milch cow.
46. Serpents and reptiles that bite sharp, hide themselves in caves and cavities in winter. These and other biting insects proliferate during the rains. Let these not come too near to us. Grant us, O' Earth! all that is auspicious and beneficial.
47. It is this, thy broad bosom, O' Mother Earth! that makes room for myriads of paths and tracks, both for pedestrians and carriages of men and materials, treaded by the cultured and the wicked. Let us succeed in driving away the wicked, the oppressor, the enemy. [Translator's Note: *Dasyu* = Name of a class of evil beings or demons, enemies

of dignitaries and men, and slain by Indra (mostly Vedic in this sense), Apte.]

49. Tigers, lions, hyenas, wolves, bears, fiends and rapacious beasts, many are the harmful and carnivorous that roam around your woodlands. Drive them all, O' Earth! far away from our homes.

52. Well-ordered are thy light and darkness, thy days and nights. Thou art often covered at places, with clouds that rain. Grant us peace and pleasure in each of our homes, O' Mother Earth!

53. The sky, the environ and the land, all have granted me width of mind (Translator's Note: *Praśasta sthāna* = literally, wide space). The fire, the sun, the waters and all the dignitaries have endowed me with wisdom and far-sight.

54. I am the victor. I am the uncommon, the most evolved on earth with potentials, unlimited. I prevail over all, everywhere at all times.

57. The racing horse raises a dust that spreads out. Spread out alike are men all around the earth. The sustaining capacity of the earth also expands fast, to uphold in its wide bosom, the woods, the trees, the shrubs and the creepers.

58. Let my speech be sweet and lovely. Let all that I see be my darling. But let me be also ferocious to destroy any one who invades.

59. Pour down thy blessings on me, O' Mother Earth! with inexhaustible milk and honey of thy breast, the abode of infinite peace, beatitude and beauty.

60. Oblations in his hands, the Architect-of-the-world (*Viśvakarmā*) invites the earth. It then emerges glowing in brilliant light along with its environs, from beneath the ocean with its land-scape, like a ship loaded with sustenances for all who get it as their mother.
61. Thou art the boat that rescues and upholds all creatures in deep see. Mother thou art to all that live. Fulfillst thou all the hopes, desires and aspirations of everyone here. Thy expanse is vast, far and wide. All thy shortfalls have been made good by Prajāpati, born of timeless Order (*Ṛta*).
62. Let all that comes from thy broad bosom be useful and helpful to us, let all these be free from any deficiency and let none of these be discarded as useless. Grant us a fully conscious long life on thy bosom, enable us to sing the song of thy excellence, O' Mother Soil!
63. With all thy blessings hold me firm, close to thy wide bosom, hold me firm well-established with all the wealth, brilliance and firmness. Thou art my wise mother O' Soil! (Translator's Note: The word '*Bhūmi*', although renderd by us as 'earth' and 'soil', also means, 'earth', 'field', 'ground', 'soil', 'site', 'receptacle', 'foundation'. It occurs to us that the word has been used in all these senses in the whole of the 'song' and not merely in the sense of the physical earth or soil. It is the impartite logical ground, the axiomatic foundation that logically sustains linguistic usage.)

We have already indicated how appealing is the poetic excellence of this sublime architecture like that of the Koṇārka temple. It is an 'impartite creative beauty' (*akhaṇḍita-rocanā-rekha*) in the words of Upendra Bhanja. We have, therefore, placed a prose rendering of almost the whole of the poem before we partition it to take up an analytical appraisal of its various strands of thought. We will now study some of its different constituent components of ideas. We will see from the study that this is an attempt at reiterating the truths that came to light, in the three preceding Vedas, the Ṛk, the Śāma and the Yajus. On close scrutiny of the linguistic expressions used in the Atharva Veda one can clearly see that this Veda was conceived long after the preceding three. The sage here intends, once again, to place in clear relief, the ideals of the *Saṁhitā* age, before the society, seeing that the latter had strayed away from those ideals. No question can arise concerning a creator or a creation out of nothing, says the Ṛgveda. The same idea is reiterated here. There has to be a creator for the creator if a creator is necessary for everything. A concept of absolute creation is meaningless and untenable in this sense. The sage here, therefore, refrains from raising this absurd question. He reiterates the concept of 'evolution', instead, already presented in the preceding Vedas.

The first and the seventh verses highlight the stream of societal evolution. The first verse contends that consequent upon their dedication (*dīkṣā*) into order (*ṛta*), truth (*satya*) and penance (*tapaḥ*), men firmly hold on to and nurture the earth as a spacious habitation, without depleting its potentials. The seventh verse similarly says that the dignitaries (*deva*) had struggled and had thereby initiated men into the ideal that they must always struggle, not only to protect the earth from being depleted of its vitality, but also to promote its sustainable deployment in more and more efficient ways. It is only when the earth is well protected that we can derive therefrom palatable vegetations and food grains for our good health and balanced physique.

Man's gratitude to the sun, to fire and to water is acknowledged, in the same vein, in the fifty third verse, appreciating their invaluable contributions in facilitating growth of discriminating intellect that is at the root of man's societal and ethical evolution.

The fifth, sixth, eighth, fifteenth and fifty-ninth verses serve, to clearly bring out the sage's vision of the stream of the geographical evolution of the earth, and to reiterate similar visions of the preceding Vedas as well. In the fifth verse the sage emphasizes that the dignitaries and the common men were born on this earth. Whatever they achieved was on this earth that is the appropriate field of action of all the dignitaries, as well as, of all the manes. It is here that the manes were born and had brought up their progenies with great care and compassion, thereby opening up the path of future progress. It is thus that they deserve all our trust and veneration (*śraddhā*). The dignitaries have, likewise, contributed to protection of our dharma, of our society and of our culture, having, once and for all, effectively eliminated all the adversaries, the demons, the *vṛtras* and the snakes (*ahi*) (Translator's Note: By logically discriminating between sustaining and degrading characters and by conducting themselves in support of the former and for elimination of the latter). They all well deserve our full-throated eulogies. The sixth verse distinctly observes that the earth bears all the minerals in its golden womb. It also bears fire. All our welfare is rooted in fire. It is the source of intellect, of light, and of warmth. It thus deserves all our eulogies. The dignitaries such as Indra, Ṛṣabha and others have ensured protection to all, and have thereby ushered in all possibilities of ample abundance on this earth. On this earth land was initially submerged in water and through a process of evolution lands gradually emerged up from the seas segregating the continents from the oceans, pronounces the eighth verse. This is an accurate reiteration of the concept of the stream of the evolutionary emergence highlighted earlier in 'The Verse to the Person', in 'The Verse to Knowledge', and in the stories of birth of the dignitaries, of the Ṛgveda. This verse, similarly brings out the point that the sages were aware of the concept of evolutionary emergence. This variegated earth was initially mere 'Being' (*sattā*), its various facets indistinct (i.e., no one has created it). What was invisible, gradually evolved out distinct and became the multifaceted visible world of knowledge. All the future developments are potentially latent as imperishable possibilities (*amṛtatva lābhara saṁbhāvanā*) in the gradual evolution of the human society. By sustainable cultivation of the earth we derive strength and virility from its nutritious food and palatable vegetations. In the same vein the fifteenth verse pronounces that bipeds and quadrupeds came out to be sustained by grasses and grains that grow up gradually through this evolutionary process. All these live, move and have their being on this mother earth. In the same evolutionary process, humanity surpassed others in working out its processes of education, culture, civilization and agriculture. Let people of five cultures be inspired by the ideal of mutual cooperation to live here in peace for ever. Cultured humanity has thus gradually spread out everywhere. Similarly, in the fifty-ninth verse, the sage seeks out the endless blessings of the earth that was the abode of infinite peace and the store house of inexhaustible supply of milk and honey.

These Vedic *āryas* were peace-loving. They knew that all welfare and progress was possible only when peace prevailed all-round. We had occasions to mention about this love of peace in many contexts in the foregoing chapters. The idea is pronounced again here in the Atharva Veda. This strand of thought comes clearly out from a scrutiny of Verses 32, 36, 37, 41, 45 and 52. In Verse 32, the sage finds that people wish to live in peace in all directions, East, West, North and South. Let there be no aggression from any quarter. Let there be no need for sharp and lethal weapons. Let the swindlers and imposters find no opportunity to attack.

Likewise, it is said in the Verse 36, that people may enjoy abundant resources round the year in all seasons. There should be no occasion for them to suffer a wretched life of scarcity of war times. Verse 37 finds that truth and righteousness (*dharma*) always prevail on this earth over untruth and perversity. The earth, because of its determined adherence to Indra, the ordainer of order and truth, has been able to dispel and discard the life-negating *vṛtra*. The earth does never swerve from truth nor does ever support untruth. In the same spirit, laments Verse 41, it is unfortunate that war-cries and war-drums do still roar around the earth. The Vedic sage exhorts people to live in peace without enemies having driven the latter far away. Verse 45 acknowledges that people talk various tongues and perform multifarious duties, display diverse cultures and features. The verse wishes these diversities not to collide but to coalesce for an overall robust life of abundance. Verse 52 also finds that light and darkness, days and nights and rains and sunshine, all are well-ordered on the earth. It wishes that people may remain well-insulated against excessive rains and scorching solar heat, and that there may prevail peace and pleasure at each and every home at all times.

Verse 35 ordains that it was suicidal to invite environmental disequilibrium by mindless depletion of forests and other natural resources. It is necessary to replenish the mining cavities and to plant a tree if one is felled. Tear not the bosom of the earth. Deplete not its life-sustaining vitality.

All the Vedas, the Ṛk, the Śāma, the Yajuḥ and the Atharva, have emphatically asserted that the Vedic *ārya* (cultured) consciously strives for a healthy and long life always supported by an abundance of resources. The idea is reiterated here in Verses 44, 62 and 63. The Atharva Veda ordains here that people should strive to live long, active and industrious lives with an abundance of wealth by appropriately utilizing the minerals and metals such as gold, steel, etc., and other natural resources preserved in the earth's mines.

All the four Vedas pronounce again and again, clear and loud, that a life alone, free from calamities, ailments and wants, was the prime objective of the Vedic *ārya*, and was the best that is desirable for humankind. They wish to keep away from calamities by effectively dispelling violent beasts such as tigers and lions, sharp biters like vipers and scorpions and harmful and wicked men. This is the idea enshrined in Verses 46, 47 and 49.

Verses 14 and 58 lay down the concept of elimination of enemies. The Vedic *ārya* never looks back from any heroic and ferocious fight to effectively vanquish the invader, the wicked who obstructs the path of evolutionary progress towards a life of abundance and bliss. Their wish for peace was concurrent with a lasting preparedness for war without any laxity at any time.

Verses 11 and 54 promulgate the victory of the culture of the Vedic *āryas*. They went ahead along the path of gradual evolution having laid aside their initial primitivity and having been initiated into the values of order (*ṛta*), truth (*satya*) and austere-penance (*tapaḥ*). They came out victorious in their struggle to live, sustained by an expansion of intellect and knowledge in a life of self-control ordained by order and truth. This process of evolutionary growth constitutes their victorious march in their struggle to live. They saw that some animals became gradually extinct whereas humanity expands in all directions. The earth upholds me 'unslain unhurt and un-subdued', announces Verse 11, giving expression to this joy of victory of the conscious humanity. 'I am the victor. I am the uncommon ... I prevail over all ...', declares Verse 54, highlighting the same joy of human evolution. (Translator's Note: The rest of the verses may be seen as expressive, explanatory or corroborative of one or the other of the aforesaid ideas.)

Our Conclusions

On a close study of the four Vedas we come to the conclusion that the Vedic culture cognizes no Creator. The Vedas propound no theory of creation. The 'Person' with a thousand heads, hands and eyes of 'The Verse to the Person' connotes 'humanity' as a conscious societal cultural entity. Living an orderly life in a group, men evolve linguistic usage, like lighting a lamp, of communicable knowledge, that was possible only in an organized societal life. Knowledge comes out, lives and goes on evolving through mutually communicative linguistic expressions. This contributes to an overall enrichment of human life. This thousand headed 'Person' is neither the 'Creator' of the world nor its sustainer. It is no God, the Omnipotent. This Person, i.e., the human society emerging from knowledge and understanding, came to be gradually seen in four pragmatic segments in accordance with the professional occupations of its members. 'Humanity' prevails, becomes time-less (immortal), declare the Vedas, on account of its initiation into the values of order, truth, penance and steadfastness, consequent upon the immortal efforts of its ideal predecessors who taught them to sacrifice their harmful, selfish, brutal, primitive instincts, as in sacrificial ceremonies. Those who hold the thousand-headed 'Person' to be the Creator and sustainer 'God' have missed to appreciate the logical meaning of the Vedas. It is illogical to conceive that the brāhmaṇa, the kṣatriya, the vaiśya and the śūdra were given birth to by the 'Person', all by himself through his speech-organ (mouth), arms, thighs and feet, respectively. The Vedas uphold that men came to be broadly categorised into four types in accordance with their respective dominant professional occupations proliferating with the evolutionary growth of multiplicity and more and more refinement of knowledge and skills and of consequential technologies. Humanity consisting of many individuals is said to have thousands of heads, eyes and hands. The broad quadruple professional categorization of societal men resulting from growth and refinement of knowledge and skills, intends to propound no theory of creation. The Vedic sage was aware that the meanings of his expressions were likely to be distorted over time. He therefore often says, "We describe the point carefully and hope that people later will see the point that we do". They often caution against a possible distortion of the meaning conveyed by means of linguistic expressions. The idea that the Vedas are impersonal (*apauruṣeya*) has definitely been distorted later. Each verse states at the start, the name of the sage who is the author thereof. It is thus blatantly erroneous to say that no man is the author of these verses. Vedas are impersonal in the sense that their truths are valid for ever. Truth cannot be worked out by anyone. It talks of a case as it is. That a statement is true, owes nothing to anyone who makes or takes it. Vedic truths are impersonal in this sense. These truths have been very critically examined and refined by many wise men before being accepted as such. An individual does not generate the truth of a statement. A statement is true irrespective of the person who utters or hears the statement. Truth of a statement conforms to what is the case. Even after the death of the speaker of a statement it is received as true if it is so. What is true is so at all times. Even if no one utters a statement its truth value is not affected. It is in this sense that the Vedic truths are impersonal (*apauruṣeya*). Like-wise it is blatantly incorrect to say that the sages are only seers and not the authors of the verses. The word 'seer' is not used here in a loose sense. 'Seer' is one who comes to know of a truth through various methods of knowledge. 'Seeing', say, of a perceptual knowledge is valid-knowledge (*prameya*) arising from appropriate application of the relevant sense organ. Perceptual valid knowledge comes from sense-experience. A 'seer' is not one who merely sees a thing already placed there by God. He is a knower. He acquires knowledge. He realizes knowledge and then presents it to others for their critical scrutiny. Truth gets established only after such critique by others from many angles. The Vedas are no divine commandments for benefits of men. It is not that the sage sees the truth already established by God.

It is often observed that without understanding the meanings of linguistic expressions some people explain distorted meanings. There are even some teachers who do not understand the meanings of sentences, but explain distorted meanings to their pupils. These are teachers of the lowest caliber. Muni Vidyāraṇya of the fourteenth century finds that there can be six types of people who are likely to get and or give out such distortions. They are (i) those of inaudible voice, (ii) singers, (iii) fast speakers, (iv) head-swingers, (v) mere readers of scripts and (vi) those who do not understand the meanings. There are those who give out the text without understanding their meanings. They have got the text by heart without appropriate appreciation. They lack conviction. So they mix up the point and speak out in very low and inaudible voice. Secondly, there are others who are unable to meet questions and to avoid discussions they quickly sing out the text, lest they may forget the chain of what is got by heart. The third type quickly speak out what is got by heart. They are fast speakers. Fourthly, there are others who, without understanding the point at issue try to speak out something while swinging their heads and throwing up their hands in various directions. They are head-swingers. The fifth type are those who merely read out from books or notes. They do not understand what they read out. The sixth type are those who not only miss the meanings but also preach distorted meanings. It is thus emphasized that one who does not understand the meanings of Vedic verses should refrain from teaching them lest the society abounds in foolish members. [Translator's Note: Vidyāraṇya's *Vivaraṇa Prameya Saṅgraha* quotes the following verse as of Prabhākara School to categorize pupils' deficiencies. Our author utilizes it to describe teachers of low caliber as well.

> *Gītī, Śīghrī, Śiraḥ-kampī,*
> *tathā likhita-pāṭhakāḥ,*
> *anarthajño, alpakaṇṭhaḥ ca*
> *ṣaḍete pāṭhakādhamāḥ.*
> (V.P.S., Amar Publications, Varanasi, 1999, p. 480)]

There is a definite reason for distortions of meanings of Vedic verses, in the style of expression of the *Saṁhitā* age. It was the convention to express many coherent ideas in the fewest possible number of words. All words of feminine gender are called as 'ladies' (*yoṣā*). When one carries a fire-pot using his/her ten fingers (Finger = *aṅguli*, feminine gender), the Vedic sage says that the pot is carried by ten ladies. Similarly, 'a person with six fingers' means, 'humanity consisting of six different cultures'. Here human cultures are fingers and there the fingers are ladies. For the Vedas the word *'ātman'* connotes the 'discriminating faculty' that distinguishes between what is right and what is wrong arising out of orderly living. This *ātman* has been gifted to men by Indra by initiating them into an orderly life style. The *ātman*, like wealth, and knowledge, can be gifted and accepted. This is no creator, sustainer Supreme Being. It goes with the death of the individual. It can, however, be immortal if it is actuated with a societal awareness. The *ātman*, i.e., the discriminating faculty of the society is immortal. The society evolves and expands. Animals become extinct due to lack of this discriminating faculty. That is how one born to human society is addressed as the progeny of immortality (*amṛtasya putraḥ*). This expression 'progeny of immortality' has no other secret meaning. One may succeed in appropriately interpreting the *Saṁhitā* literature if one keeps the latter's style of expression constantly in view.